TABLE MAGIC

how to create fabulous table settings

TABLE MAGIC

Tessa Evelegh

PHOTOGRAPHY BY Polly Wreford

aqua marine

This edition is published by Aquamarine

Aquamarine is an imprint of Anness Publishing Ltd
Hermes House, 88–89 Blackfriars Road, London SE1 8HA
tel. 020 7401 2077; fax 020 7633 9499
www.aquamarinebooks.com; info@anness.com

UK agent: The Manning Partnership Ltd
tel. 01225 478 444; fax 01225 478 440; sales@manning–partnership.co.uk

UK distributor: Grantham Book Services Ltd
tel. 01476 541080; fax 01476 541061; orders@gbs.tbs–ltd.co.uk

North American agent/distributor: National Book Network
tel. 301 459 3366; fax 301 429 5746; www.nbnbooks.com

Australian agent/distributor: Pan Macmillan Australia
tel. 1300 135 113; fax 1300 135 103; customer.service@macmillan.com.au

A CIP catalogue record for this book is available from the British Library.

Publisher: JOANNA LORENZ
Senior Editor: CLARE NICHOLSON
Designer: LISA TAI
Photography: POLLY WREFORD
Illustrator: ANNA KOSKA

Previously published as *Table Settings*

10 9 8 7 6 5 4 3 2 1

CONTENTS

THE TABLE SETTINGS 56

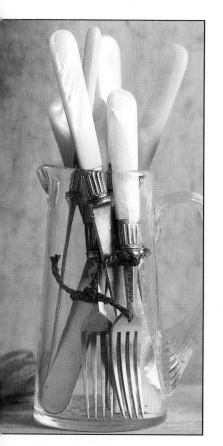

INTRODUCTION

Much of the enjoyment of inviting friends and family to join you for a meal is the pleasure of preparing it; of making the table and room look inviting, as well as cooking delicious food. A beautifully laid table provides an inviting ambience that both welcomes the guests and sets off the meal. The basic ingredients of crisp linen, fine crockery, glass and cutlery are always there, but with some imagination they can be set off in very different ways, depending on how you treat them and the decorations you use. The fold of the napkins, the choice of serving dishes, flowers, candles and candlesticks, and the presentation of the food, all make a fundamental difference to the overall look of the table. The ideas throughout this book do not require you to buy expensive pieces of tableware, or to replace what you already have. Using everyday items and a basic dinner service, you can create very different table settings to suit the mood and the occasion and to lend an individual feel to your table.

THE HISTORY OF TABLE SETTINGS

Sitting down to a table laid with a plate and a battery of utensils for each person is a fairly modern innovation. As recently as the fifteenth century, there were no forks and "messmates" (those who shared plates) tackled food only with knives. Once the fork arrived, however, it opened the floodgates to a whole range of

● Below: *The need to eat together is so fundamental that it has been immortalized in religious symbolism. This illumination from a 14th Century psalter is reminiscent of the Lord's Last Supper.*

utensils, designed for use with different kinds of food. These included fish knives and forks, soup spoons, pickle forks, cake knives, jam spoons and so on. By Edwardian times, elaborate utensils and a complicated code of behaviour turned formal mealtimes into an assault course for many, especially if they were not in their usual social circle. Thankfully, this prissiness has all but disappeared and cutlery and crockery sets are now far more streamlined. The way we use them is more flexible, too. Mixing and matching crockery and linens is now acceptable, offering scope for creating imaginative and individual table settings.

CREATING MOOD

As well as laying a table and arranging the items on it, you need to set the mood for the meal. One of the most successful ways to plan this in advance is to make a checklist of all five senses – sight, hearing, smell, taste and touch – and to make sure that each one is satisfied.

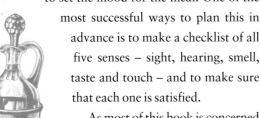

As most of this book is concerned with the look of the table settings, you will find plenty of inspiration for visual appeal. Do not overlook lighting. You need to strike a balance between a moody and a gloomy effect. A few spotlights or wall lights around the room should provide enough ambient light without being over-bright. Avoid a central pendant light flooding the whole room, as this could be too stark. Candles provide the most flattering way to light the table and the people around it. Candles also give enormous scope for decoration, as candle holders can be bought or made in any number of different ways to add impact to the table.

Music is one of the best mood-setters. With the volume turned up just enough so that it can be heard, but not so much that it will drown the conversation, it will gloss over any awkward silences and encourage lively conversation. This is especially important when everyone first arrives and needs a little warming up.

Hopefully, the food itself will produce some mouth-watering aromas, but activating the sense of smell does not have to stop there. Richly scented flowers or herbs and aromatic candles can all contribute to a perfectly perfumed dining room. Your menu will stimulate the taste buds, but you could also offer tasty morsels, set in bowls around the table, for guests to nibble between courses.

● Above: *The Romans turned banqueting into an art form, eating and drinking together for many hours, as recorded in this 16th Century Florentine painting.*

Finally, items such as crisp linen napkins, silky tablecloths and tactile party favours all contribute to making a table feel nice to the touch. Party favours, especially, add a personal touch that will delight the guests. Often filled with sweets or small gifts, these can be enjoyed at the end of the meal, or taken home to be unwrapped later.

ETIQUETTE

No matter how easy-going we might consider ourselves to be, or how old-fashioned etiquette appears to us, we all conform to an etiquette within our own social circle. Etiquette is really another word for manners, which are simply a set of rules developed so that everyone instinctively knows what to do in certain situations and can therefore be comfortable within the group. Manners are constantly changing, however, and certainly social etiquette is no longer as rigid as it used to be. The overriding point of good manners is to be considerate to others and to make them feel at ease, and this is no less true at the table.

LAYING THE TABLE

Formal tables are laid according to traditional etiquette, the purpose behind the ordered positioning of all the items being the smooth running of the meal. More informal meals certainly do not have to adhere rigidly to the rules: indeed, many restaurants "break the rules" to create more imaginative settings. You will find plenty of inspiration for such ideas in the second half of the book. But for now, the following is the correct way to lay a formal table.

● Above: *This formal setting shows (working inwards) forks on the left for fish, meat and salad; and on the right, the soup spoon and knives for fish, meat and cheese. The dessert spoon and fork are above the plate.*

MATS OR CLOTH?

If you have a table with a fine polished surface, you may well want to show it off by using table mats, and that is acceptable. It is also perfectly correct to put a cloth on a table for a formal dinner. Traditionally, this is white, though nowadays coloured cloths are also used.

CUTLERY

Cutlery should be laid on either side of the plates so that implements for the first course are on the outside, with those for subsequent courses arranged so that diners can work in towards the plates as each course arrives. Forks go on the left side and knives on the right. If the first course needs just a fork, this will be put on the outside at the left, despite the fact that most guests will use it in their right hand. Butter knives may be put on side plates, and dessert spoons and forks may be placed on either side of the table mat or above it.

GLASSES

Where just one glass is used, this should be placed above the knife or knives. Where more than one is used, these can be arranged in order from left to right or from right to left, or in a triangular pattern above the knife. It is correct to set all the glasses on the table before the meal begins. However, if there is not enough space, port and liqueur glasses can be brought to the table when they are needed at the end of the meal.

Glasses for different drinks are usually of different sizes. They go up in this order: liqueur, port, sherry, white wine, red wine, water. Champagne should be sipped from tall, slender glasses, not wide, shallow ones. Water can be served in a tumbler. It is normal nowadays to provide glasses for water and a jug of water at every meal.

PLATES

The bread-and-butter plate is placed to the left of the place setting. Warm plates are brought to the table as they are needed. If the starter is cold, it can be placed on the table before the guests are invited to be seated.

● Above: *Cutlery is placed on either side of the plates in order of courses from the outside in, so that guests automatically know which implements to use for which dish.*

CONDIMENTS AND SERVERS

Salt and pepper containers should be placed on the table at regular intervals so that they are within easy reach of everyone. Servers should be laid within reach of the serving dishes.

SEATING PLAN

If equal numbers of men and women are present, they should be seated alternately in a way that the host and hostess feel will make for the best conversation. Place cards can be used if desired or needed. For very formal dinners, the whole name of the guest, including the title, should be used: Dr, Mrs, Miss, Ms, Mr. On less formal occasions, using just the first name is equally correct.

SERVING

Each guest should be served from the left. Although a formal dinner will probably be attended by a number of servants, this is not viable for most of us, so pass the dishes around from the left, instead. This leaves the right hand of each of the guests free to do the helping.

CLEARING

It is correct to clear the table of everything to do with the main course – including condiments – before serving dessert.

THE ELEMENTS

Setting the table can be like creating a still-life – the more beautiful the

components, the more attractive the finished result.

EXPLORING THE ELEMENTS

China, glass, cutlery and linens together make up the overall look of any setting. On to that framework can be added candles and their holders plus the table decorations, which are the icing on the cake. These are obviously areas where you can add personal touches that may be quite different from anyone else's, and even very different each time you entertain. But with imagination and flair, you can be creative with all the elements that go into laying a table.

Your existing tableware will have the greatest influence on the table settings you create. You will probably instinctively choose designs that suit the style of your home, whether it is elegantly modern, traditional or has a more relaxed country look. Given this starting point, however, there is no reason why your table has to look the same each time you set it. With very little (and sometimes no) extra effort, you can make it seem quite different every time. Of course, you may have a favourite look, and there is no reason why you should not want always to re-create it. But there will be occasions, such as Christmas, Easter or at special celebrations, when you wish to make your table look more special than usual. The other main reasons for wanting to adapt the look of your table settings are that, as time goes by, fashions in home style change

and personal tastes develop. You may want to reflect these changes in your table settings.

This section of the book will help you make your initial choices. For each element, there is a directory to point you in the direction most likely to suit your own style. The directory is shown mostly in neutral colours, not because they are

● Above: *A large jug for cool, soft summer drinks is given elegant embellishment with a frosted lime pattern.*

● Left : *The simple combination of pine, clay pots and cream earthenware, warmed by soft candlelight, makes for an inviting ambience.*

considered to be any better or more correct, but simply because colour and pattern would have dominated the material types and shapes. Once you know what type of china or glass, for example, you prefer, you will find it easier to decide on particular designs, shades and patterns. You can find inspiration for these details in the table-setting styles shown in the second part of the book.

Once you have selected the elements of the table settings, there are many very simple ways in which they can be used to different effect. You can mix and match colours, fold napkins in various ways, or use differently coloured candles, for example. Or, with a little extra effort, you can make alternative napkin

● Above: *Plain white china on brightly checked cloths lends a holiday feel to a summer breakfast setting.*

rings from ribbon, raffia or string, perhaps adding a flower or leaf for decoration. You can frost glasses, and add a selection of beads to linens. You can tie or wrap up cutlery, stand it in glasses or lay it on plates. In fact, whether you like stitching, stamping, tying, wrapping, frosting, beading, flower arranging or simply mixing and matching, you will find many ideas that will help you to choose and adapt every element of any table setting in this section.

CHINA

China creates the single greatest impact on table settings – not just in terms of COLOUR AND PATTERN, but in the material it is made of and in the form of the designs. Many people build up two dinner services – an ELEGANT DESIGN for dinner parties, and a more everyday set for FAMILY MEALS. But this need not limit anyone to just two table setting looks;

you can use these as a FRAMEWORK around which to build endless styles to suit every occasion. You could buy some pretty hand-painted soup bowls or side plates to CO-ORDINATE with your main dinner services. Or you could add a single beautiful salad bowl, dessert dish or soup tureen to give your table an elegant new look. Bearing this in mind, choose the MAIN DINNER SET very carefully in a colour or pattern that you will not tire of easily, but will continue to love for many years.

● Right: *Look for pieces with elegant flowing lines. Good shape enhances all china, regardless of colour or pattern.*

CHINA CHOICES

Plates and dishes do not have to be made of china. You can just as well eat off metal, glass, wood or plastic, and all of these materials enrich the look of a table setting. However, most plates and dishes are made from some form of ceramic, now known as china because in the eighteenth century a high proportion of ceramics were imported from China. There are four main types: earthenware, stoneware, porcelain and bone china.

Earthenware is made from clay that has been baked hard. It is very porous, and so has to be glazed to make it suitable for use with food and liquid. In the Mediterranean region, sometimes only the insides and part of the outsides of bowls and plates are glazed, using bright colours to contrast with the natural tones of the still-exposed earthenware. By contrast, English earthenware is traditionally fully glazed and, sometimes, highly decorated. The result is attractive everyday china in elegant flowing shapes.

Stoneware, fired at a higher temperature than earthenware and then vitrified, is very hard-wearing. Not usually patterned, it became popular in northern Europe.

Porcelain, invented by the Chinese in about the seventh century, is considered to be the finest ceramic. There are two kinds. Hard paste is made of china clay (kaolin) mixed with finely ground stone, and is fired at extremely high temperatures. The other kind is soft paste. It is made from china clay mixed with sand, lime or soda, and versions were made in Sèvres and Limoges, in France. Porcelain has a translucent quality, and produces the most delicate and graceful of shapes. The English adapted porcelain, using china clay and bone ash to make bone china. This is also fine and translucent, though not as delicate in form as porcelain.

● Above: *The process of blue underglaze printing on earthenware was perfected in 1784 in England by Josiah Spode. The patterns were initially reproductions of Chinese porcelain designs, though new designs soon followed, three of which are still popular today: Blue Italian, Tower Blue and Willow. The appeal of these traditional designs is that they look wonderful mixed and matched.*

● Above: *China of all kinds can have relief patterns, which are created by pressing the clay into a mould during manufacture. Generally, the finer the clay, the finer the patterns, but even less delicate earthenware can be pressed into exquisite designs.*

● Left: *Earthenware makes excellent everyday tableware. It is not as fine as porcelain, so the shapes are usually simpler, and its softer consistency means it chips more easily.*

● Right: *Creamware is so-called because it has the natural creamy colour of the clay. A fine earthenware that became popular in the last century, many creamware patterns are plain, but others are very elaborate, with moulded and pierced designs.*

● Below: *Bone china was invented in the English potteries, and is still considered to be among the finest of dinnerware. The understated elegance of this design, decorated only by bands of gold, is sure to stand the test of time.*

● Above: *The fine consistency of unfired porcelain means it can be shaped into delicate flowing designs and, if the clay is used thinly, the pieces can have an exquisite translucent quality.*

FINE WAYS WITH CHINA

The art of successful table setting is to be clever with the crockery, so mix, match, adapt and adorn your dinner service to suit the mood and the occasion. According to *Debrett's Etiquette and Modern Manners*, for formal dinner parties all the china ought to match, with the exception of the dessert plates. However, few of us regularly give formal parties and the fashion nowadays is to be more relaxed and imaginative, mixing as well as matching.

The effective way to mix pieces from different sets is to link them by colour. So by collecting all white, or all cream, for example, you can create a wonderful overall effect from pieces that were not necessarily designed to match. Another way is to collect two different colours that go well together. You may choose black and white or Mediterranean blues and greens. Mix the whole service, or simply buy colour-complementing dessert plates or serving dishes. But even if you prefer to have everything matching, there are ways to give your existing china a different look. Underplates provide a lot of scope. Buy brass to lend sparkle to tables at Christmas or other celebrations, or coloured glass to add a new look on any occasion. Alternatively, you could put clear glass plates on top of those from the main set, with something decorative between, which, again, can be changed to suit the occasion.

Piles of crockery always look effective, adding extra dimension to the setting. A typical pile may consist of the underplate, plate, and the soup bowl or the starter plate.

Tables always look prettier if the china is full when the guests arrive to take their seats. So fill the top vessel – soup in the bowl, or starter on the plate. If you prefer to bring soup, steaming hot, to serve at the table, decorate each bowl with a party favour or napkin, which can be moved by the guests when the first course is served.

● Above: *Any china is given an extra dimension when it is set upon something else. This pearl-finished glass coffee cup is placed on a shell-shaped butter dish. For a celebration mood, it has been given a little glitter with silver dragées, a gold cord tie and a silver-gilt teaspoon.*

● Above: *Plates provide plenty of scope for imaginative settings. Place glass plates on underplates (or even your largest dinner plates), decorated with leaves, fabric, flowers or sweets that will show through. Here, an unsophisticated glass plate is set on skeletonized magnolia leaves laid on a frosted glass underplate for a very pretty overall effect.*

● Above: *Brass underplates put every style of china in the party mood. Here, the gold rim of the elegant porcelain soup cup picks up the brass, but even if your dinner service is plain, it will look richer if set on metal. For very special occasions, add a gold tassel and wrap party favours in gold organza tied with golden cord.*

● Left: *Creamware looks especially effective when mixed and matched. Here, the elegantly plain cup and simply bordered soup dish are set off by an intricately pierced plate. The pale lustre of mother-of-pearl cutlery handles finishes off the creamy look.*

CUTLERY

The battery of cutlery that is now available is a relatively recent innovation. DINNER FORKS for use at meals did not appear until the sixteenth century but, once they did so, it seems there was NO LOOKING BACK. Different styles of knives, spoons and forks were invented for a variety of uses until, by Edwardian times, there seemed to be MEALTIME TOOLS available for

every imaginable use. Intricate fish knives, fish forks and servers, CAKE FORKS with cutting edges, and long-handled pickle forks for spiking preserved vegetables at the bottom of deep jars all came into use. TABLE ETIQUETTE was very precise during this period, and everything had to be done properly using the right equipment. FORMAL CUTLERY, with several sizes of knife, fork and spoon, is still available, but nowadays most everyday sets simply consist of basic knives, forks, spoons and teaspoons.

● Right: *Whatever style you choose, a set of cutlery that complements the setting will enhance the look of the table.*

CLASSIC CUTLERY

Traditionally, formal cutlery was made of silver although, as this is an expensive metal, much of it was plated. The knives, and sometimes the forks, had handles made of a different material, such as bone, horn or wood. The Victorians initiated a fashion for making elaborate special-use cutlery, which may have been intricately engraved and given handles in valuable materials such as mother-of-pearl. Among these were sets of fish cutlery, cake knives and coffee spoons. Very special sets of coffee spoons were even given a silver gilt lining to their bowl. Such celebration sets are highly collectable today, especially if they are complete and in their original green baize roll.

Nowadays, everyday cutlery needs to be dishwasher proof. As machine washing can strip off silver plate and loosen handle fixings, silver-plated cutlery and bone-, wood- and horn-handled pieces are usually kept for best. Even everyday cutlery of yesteryear, made of mild steel with fixed wooden handles, would not survive the rigours of the modern dishwasher.

Most modern cutlery designs are in stainless steel, often made in one piece, handle and all. But in recent years there has been a fashion for contrasting handles, usually made from plastics and acrylic resins. Such styles can make up the main core of your cutlery, which can then be added to with special sets for fish, desserts and coffee. Beautiful pieces of serving cutlery, both antique and modern, can also greatly enhance a table setting for a special occasion.

● Above: *Wooden handles become wonderfully smoothed and polished with age, developing a patina that is hard to match in any other cutlery. However, these should not be immersed in water for more than the few seconds it takes to wash them, otherwise the handles could become loose.*

● Below: *Not all modern stainless steel cutlery has to have fast-food styling. This exquisite set verges on sculpture, with the smooth polished lines of blade, bowl and prongs contrasting dramatically with the textured rough-hewn handles.*

● Above: *The smooth cylindrical handle of this silver knife lends a modern look to the otherwise classic lines.*

● Right: *Special-purpose cutlery, such as fish knives and forks and pickle forks, was often given special treatment. The decorative silver blades and mother-of-pearl handles of these pieces are typical.*

● Above: *The knives of traditional silver-plated cutlery very often have bone handles, which mellow with age to a wonderful golden hue. However, these types of handles need to be washed with care, or they may become loose over time. Only dip them in water for the briefest time possible, and dry them thoroughly afterwards.*

● Right: *Clear acrylic resin is a marvellous modern material that is often used for handles, lending a sparkling glass-like quality to cutlery.*

CREATIVE CUTLERY

Knives, forks and spoons can have a wonderful sculptural quality to them, which may be used in many ways in a table setting. The formal and obvious way is to lay them, in accordance with etiquette, soldier-like on either side of each plate. But even on these occasions, butter knives can be laid diagonally across the side plate, and serving cutlery placed artistically anywhere on the table that is within easy reach of the serving dishes.

On buffet tables, there is more scope for creativity as it is usual to wrap the sets of cutlery in napkins and to stack these at one side of the table. Each stack can be decorated with leaves, flowers or ribbons. An alternative is to stand the cutlery in a glass, jug or vase for guests to pick out for themselves. Cutlery can also be used vertically for informal dinners and suppers, lending height to table settings, even those where the places are laid. Try standing cutlery for starters in tumblers, for example, for guests to remove when the course is served or when the glasses are filled, whichever comes first. Particularly attractive sets of cutlery can be laid on the plates, arranged decoratively in the middle, across the top or on one side.

Another idea is to adorn the cutlery itself, tying it in pairs or threes with ribbon, raffia, cord or string. You could also tie in a place card, or tuck in a flower, leaf or, if you wish, a chandelier crystal, a tassel or a shell for extra decoration.

● Above: *On buffet tables, cutlery can be put in a container for guests to pick up for themselves. This idea looks particularly effective when tones and textures are co-ordinated. Here, the natural shades and textures of wood, linen and horn blend in glorious harmony.*

● Right: *Lend interest to empty plates by laying cutlery tied with a flamboyant bow in the centre. This gold metal-shot ribbon teams perfectly with the metals of brass plate and silver knife and fork.*

● Above: *Modern brass cutlery gets special treatment at each place setting by being tied with a golden tassel and stood up in an amber glass. The pretty overall effect and complementary tones add up to a delightful place decoration.*

● Right: *Pretty cutlery deserves to be shown off, and a buffet table offers plenty of scope for a little ingenuity. These mother-of-pearl handles look wonderful en masse, so stand them in a glass jug, tied in pairs for easy retrieval as the guests collect their food.*

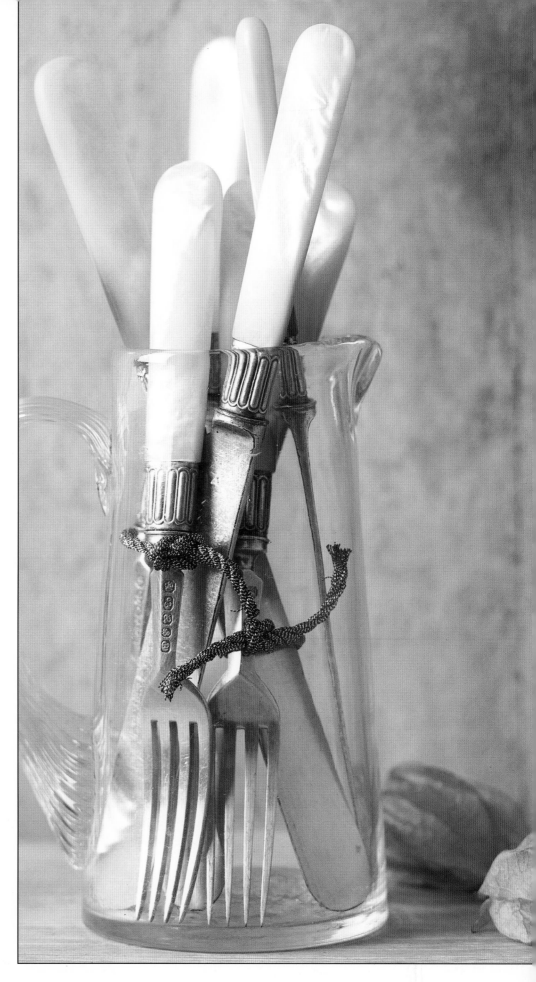

GLASS

The glorious reflective quality of glassware brings SPARKLE to every table setting. The more facets it offers to the light, the more sparkle it brings, CUT GLASS being the ultimate jewel in the table-setting crown. Teamed with the dancing light of reflected candle flames, it lends a diamond-like shimmer to the table. UNCUT GLASS also adds glisten to the

table, but in a cleaner, uncluttered way that some may even say is more ELEGANT. At its simplest, glass is represented by a single SIMPLE TUMBLER placed at the guest's right hand; for a formal dinner, this can grow to a whole group, preferably from the same glass service, though in different sizes and often different but RELATED SHAPES. These can stand, like a family at each place, gathered above the blade of the knife. If space is limited, extra glasses may need to be added as required.

● Right: *Glass lends height and sparkle to every table setting. Choose shapes that complement the main dinner service.*

A GUIDE TO GLASS

Glass at its finest is lead crystal. Feel the weight of an antique drinking glass, hand-blown and grey with lead, and you will have a yardstick by which to measure glassware. Modern glass comes in a variety of shapes with a surprisingly wide choice of finishes. You can choose the fine geometric lines of modern Swedish glass or the voluptuous curvy lines of neo-eighteenth-century shapes. If glass is cheap, it is likely to be a thicker vessel, pressed into shape in a factory. If it is very expensive, it may be hand blown. In between, it may have been manufactured in a factory where the blowing is automated.

Glass making was discovered in the third millennium BC. Ancient Greece and Byzantium produced exquisite glass that was, to some degree, imitated by the fifteenth-century Venetians. The curved bell shapes of eighteenth-century English glass marked another high point in glass manufacture, and this form is undergoing a renaissance today.

When buying glasses, choose generous sizes: small ones can look mean. Red wine and brandy glasses, especially, should be capacious as the wine needs to breathe, benefiting from the largest possible surface area.

While the dishwasher brings back the sparkle to most glass, valuable crystal should be hand washed. Decanters need to be clean inside and out. If a bottle brush cannot reach all the inner surfaces, half fill the decanter with warm water and washing-up liquid, add a handful of rice and shake. The grains of rice will gently scrub the inside of the decanter for you.

● Left: *Painted glass can be as simple as this example with white dots and golden rings, or it may be more elaborately painted with figurative images such as flowers and birds.*

● Left: *The delicate diagonal ripples on the tumbler were created by twisting the glass as it was blown. Although these two glasses are not part of the same set, their ridged hand-blown quality and their co-ordinating gold rims make them pleasingly compatible.*

● Above: *Cut crystal, like cut diamonds, is seen as precious, having a jewel-like quality. The patterns may be geometrically trellis-like, or have a more organic, flowering form.*

● Left: *Coloured glass is enjoying a revival, but usually only part of the glass is tinted. Sometimes, just a band near the top, or all or part of the stem, is coloured. The entire bowl of these glasses is tinted a wonderfully rich amber shade that would add warmth to any table setting.*

● Above: *Engraved glass has a wonderful delicate quality. Look for the finer, more detailed designs, so that you can mix and match glasses and decanters with confidence.*

● Above: *The pure geometric lines of modern Swedish designs – free of embellishment – have a special elegance that celebrates the translucent purity of glass.*

29

GREAT WAYS WITH GLASS

Glass is so beautiful in itself that it needs little decoration, but it is lovely to make something special of, say, a pre-dinner cocktail. Frosting the rim with egg white and caster sugar is a traditional idea, and one that always delights. Take this basic concept one step further by painting simple motifs like stars, hearts, spots and stripes on to the side of the glass in beaten egg white, and then shaking on the caster sugar. The patterns will stay on the glasses all evening until they are washed off with hot water and detergent.

Tequila cocktails are traditionally sipped through salt and lemon, and a frosting of salt makes a decorative solution. There are other easy tricks: try freezing tiny flowers into ice cubes and putting one in each drink. The zest of citrus fruits – lemon, lime, even orange – gives an elegant touch that is refreshingly different from the more usual fruit slices. Rather more flamboyant are the salad-like additions to a glass of Pimm's – cucumber, apple and blue-flowered borage.

Tassels, ribbons, cords, beads and even feathers can be tied decoratively around the stems of glasses, or golden wire wound around them in graceful imitation of Italian wine bottles.

Decanters, with their slim necks and curved bodies, offer yet more scope for witty decoration. Traditionally, they wear necklace-like silver name chains, so there is no reason why they should not be given more innovative "jewellery".

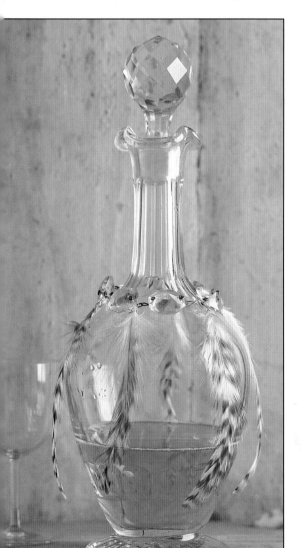

● Left: *Perennially elegant, frosted rims are easy to apply to glasses. Put beaten egg white on one saucer and caster sugar on another. Dip each glass rim into the egg white, then into the caster sugar.*

● Opposite: *An elegant way to decorate pre-dinner glasses is to wrap them with skeletonized magnolia leaves, held in place with one long stitch where the sides meet.*

● Left: *A witty reference to silver chain decanter labels can be made with a necklace. There is something wickedly sensuous about this one made of chandelier crystals and feathers. The crystals are linked with fuse wire, and the feathers have fuse-wire hooks wound on to the quills to attach them to the necklace.*

● Right: *Trim stemmed glasses with ribbon, cord, tassels or beads. These gauzy ribbons relate well to the translucency of the glass, adding a delightful finishing touch.*

LINEN

Beautiful TABLE SURFACES deserve to be shown off and, in such circumstances, it is quite correct to forgo the TABLECLOTH, choosing table mats instead. But while formal etiquette probably refers to expensive FRENCH POLISHING and burr oak, nowadays many of us love a limed or painted finish, too. Traditionally for formal dinners, a tablecloth is white

and preferably linen, and is draped to hang halfway down to the floor. More informally, sheets, bedcovers, or any other substantial length of fabric, such as a sari, can also be used to widen the repertoire for an imaginatively dressed table. Napkins may or may not match the tablecloth, and can be used as an art form in themselves. Whole books have been written about NAPKIN FOLDING, favourite styles being the mitre and lotus flower. However, when time is of the essence, simple folds are a necessity and are certainly as elegant.

● Right: *Simply folded pure-white or natural linen still makes for the most sophisticated of napkins.*

A LIST OF LINENS

Little can match the look and feel of linen. Lovely in white, even more lovely in its natural undyed state, linen's crisp line and faultless weave hangs beautifully to set off the well-laid table perfectly. Try using matching napkins, which have as their only embellishment restrained drawn threadwork decorating the hemline.

Heavy cottons, classical damasks with glossy interwoven designs, also look wonderful on tables. Originally made of silk in Damascus, the Crusaders brought damasks back to Europe where the idea was adapted to linen, although it is now more usually seen in cotton. Damasks are still favourite table coverings, and are often sold with matching napkins.

Cotton comes in many other guises: trimmed with delicate lace, embellished with elaborate cutwork, appliqué or embroidery, or simply woven in homespun checks and bold stripes. Rich woven and printed textiles bought while on holiday abroad make fabulous table coverings, evoking the ambience of warmer climes. Another idea for creating impact inexpensively is to use deep-dyed cotton sheets, or even to tie-dye old white ones.

Silk seems an extravagant table covering, but its appearance is wonderfully rich for special occasions. If you can find inexpensive lengths, such as saris in local Asian markets, make use of them for the most glamorous table setting. The table top can be protected with an overcloth. Indeed, an overcloth of metallized fabric such as organza can enrich the whole look of the table.

At the other end of the scale, where young children are involved, plasticized cottons provide the best solution. These have become increasingly sophisticated, being produced in a variety of striped and geometric as well as floral designs. Alternatively, try paper, which is shedding its utilitarian image. The finest paper napkins used to be Japanese, with delicate designs decorating the often translucent paper. Now, Western fabric designers are producing fabulous paper tableware, which dispenses with washing and ironing while lending the table a crisp, elegant look.

● Above: *Simple cotton comes in many pretty guises: lace-edged, trimmed with drawn threadwork and embroidered in endless ways, including cutwork, as shown here, which has been popular for teatime settings since the Victorian era.*

● Above: *The crisp, permanent pleats of this contemporary off-white linen napkin are surprisingly enduring in that they can happily survive the washing machine. Pretty yet elegant, the pleats are reminiscent of a lady's evening dress.*

● Left: *Paper has moved a long way from plain colours (though these still look striking). As well as pretty floral patterns, many designers are coming up with boldly coloured geometric shapes.*

● Below: *Damask, with its glorious interwoven designs, was originally only made of silk, as with this fine example. Nowadays, it is more likely to be made of heavy white cotton.*

● Above: *In both pure white and its natural undyed state, linen is still the most elegant table textile. Choose it plain, simple and unembellished, or with a restrained border such as drawn threadwork or blanket stitch.*

● Above: *Cotton weaves from the Indian subcontinent are often checked or striped – both smart patterns that are easy to mix and match.*

INSPIRED IDEAS FOR LINENS

It is not difficult to be innovative with linens. Napkins can very easily be equipped with unusual "rings", embroidered or embellished with beads. Tablecloths can be trimmed in endless ways, can be given overcloths or can even be stencilled, stamped, appliquéd or embroidered.

Napkins are obviously the easiest linens to use creatively. While the fashion for elaborate folding is difficult to equate with the busy lives most of us lead, there are many quick and effective ways of making simple folds. The aim is to relate the size of the folded napkin to the plate it is lying on. Small tea napkins may be folded into squares or triangles, while larger dinner napkins could be left as oblongs. Another smart idea is to roll them into sausages or to scrunch them into soft pleats. If you plan to do this, first fold the napkin until its length fits the plate. You may do this by folding it in half widthways before

"pleating", or you may need to make a large tuck in the middle, even after folding, to make the napkin fit the plate. Napkin rings can be made from any material: cord, ribbon or raffia, leather thongs, mini-herbal wreaths or even leaves. You can then tuck in flowers, leaves, berries or feathers for decoration.

Both napkins and cloths can be made special with trimmings such as tassels or beads at corners, fringes, or even fraying to soften the edges. Less obvious trimmings, such as buttons and shells, pebbles and even twigs can also be used.

Tablecloths do not necessarily have to have been purpose-made. Any suitable length of fabric – bedspreads, saris, sheeting or curtain lining – will do. When a fabric is not too expensive, you can embellish it with stamps, stencils or fabric paint; alternatively, try one of these decorations on a cheap fabric – such as white muslin – laid over a white cloth.

● Below: *Evocative of American Indian dress, a leather thong bound round and round natural linen, then trimmed with game feathers, looks fabulous. To create this look, fold the napkin into quarters, scrunch it together corner to corner, then bind it in the middle.*

● Above: *This napkin is actually a linen tea towel, which has been rolled up diagonally, then used to tie up a soup bowl and plate. Such a charming idea is easy to co-ordinate as blue-banded café china is not difficult to find and perfectly matches the classic blue-and-white tea towel.*

● Right: *Even leaves can be turned into napkin rings. Here, two small ornamental cabbage leaves have been pinned together using two small twigs. The corners of the napkin were folded to the middle, then the napkin was folded in half and scrunched in the middle to make a neat bow effect.*

● Below: *To make this unusual napkin ring, fold a leather thong four times, passing the loop through the hole of a large bead or button, then thread the loose ends through this. Next, pass the "tail" around the napkin, over the thong attached to the bead or button and to the back, then tie it to fix. If you cannot find an ornament exactly like this one, use any large toggle instead.*

CANDLES

Candles are still the most pleasing form of table lighting, casting a natural FLATTERING GLOW over table and diners alike. Their dancing flames have a beguiling quality that no light bulb could begin to imitate, and their evocative waxy aroma immediately creates a ROMANTIC AMBIENCE. Scented candles will enhance the mood further. Choose from the many aromatherapy perfumes available to suit the spirit of the

occasion. Candles come in many SHAPES and forms, but even with ordinary dinner candles you can create many different looks to suit the table setting. COLOUR CO-ORDINATE them with the tablecloth or china and put them in holders that are in keeping with the overall style. Whether you choose a CLASSIC CANDELABRA or a discreet modern holder, be sure to position the candles where they will not dazzle the diners.

● Right: *The choice of candle holder lends style: discreet modern holders make as large a statement as flamboyant candelabras.*

ALL KINDS OF CANDLES

The elegant tapered shapes of traditional dipped candles evoke a bygone era that is appealing in any table setting. However, it is ironic that we are now prepared to pay premium prices for this look, which was originally the result of the manufacturing process rather than any design ideal. It was not until stearin was developed, early in the nineteenth century, that candles could be moulded into almost any shape, including the straight-sided church pillar candles. This style, in restrained creamy white, is still acceptable for absolutely any occasion, along with beeswax, with its golden honey-scented and softly textured quality.

Today, candles have become decorative features in themselves, and there is much more choice. They are moulded into almost any form, and manufacturers are catering for every taste. At Christmas, you can decorate the table with Father Christmas, snowman or Christmas pudding candles; for other occasions, you can find candles in the shape of fruits, vegetables, feathers, simple pyramids or even architectural mouldings. There are also decorated candles: those that have surface decoration, such as carving or applied dried herbs and flowers, and those that have patterns that run all through the wax, such as the so-called stained-glass candles that mimic Venetian *millefiore* mosaic glass.

There are also floating candles, some of which are simple spherical shapes while others resemble flowers. In low bowls of water, these give out a gentle light.

● Above: *Candles are made in any number of shapes, from children's novelties to fruits and flowers. Set on a plate, they provide the table with an alternative source of low light.*

● Above: *An increasing number of candles are sold in a variety of containers. Oyster shells have a wonderful textural quality that provides an interesting contrast to the smooth wax.*

● Above: *Glass oil lamps have become a popular way of bringing flickering flames to the table. They are available in a variety of shapes and sizes, and there is a choice of clear, golden or deep blue oil to burn in them. Delightful on their own, they look spectacular when grouped into a display.*

● Right: *The evocative natural aroma of beeswax makes these candles universally appealing. They are expensive, though much slower-burning than the more common paraffin candles. Beeswax usually comes in thin sheets, and the candles are rolled into straight-sided or conical beehive shapes.*

● Below: *Floating candles look charming in glass bowls. As well as spherical shapes, flowers, fish, stars and suns are readily available.*

● Above: *Classic straight-sided church pillar candles come in many sizes: from a slender 2.2cm/⅞in to a chunky 7.5cm/3in diameter; from a petite 15cm/6in to a lofty 60cm/24in height. Containing a mixture of beeswax and paraffin wax, their burning time is longer than average – between seven and 220 hours.*

CLEVER WAYS WITH CANDLES

Once you have chosen your candles, there are many clever ways to adapt them and their holders to make even more imaginative displays for the table.

You can decorate the candles themselves, by spraying paint through stencils to make designs, by carving patterns in them, or by sticking dried herbs and flowers to their surface using melted wax. Alternatively, you can take a more organic route, tying leaves or sticks around them, or even studding them with spices such as cloves.

Another idea is to make your own candles in organic or unusual "holders" by slowly melting wax in a double boiler over a low heat and pouring it into your chosen container. Try this with brightly coloured tins, garden pots, heavy glasses, shells, or even fruit or vegetable skins. Small candles in low holders like these look very pretty scattered around the table, lending low light that does not interfere with conversation.

An alternative way to use candle light centrally without dazzling the diners is to float candles in a glass bowl hung above the table. Glass hanging lanterns imported from India are perfect for the purpose. Or suspend traditional lanterns, either singly or in a group. When buying lanterns, make sure they are solidly made: some cheap imports are constructed from softer metals that grow very hot and may cause the solder to melt, which can be extremely dangerous.

Candelabras, candlesticks and holders can make a design statement in themselves, becoming a table centrepiece. They can also be adapted to suit the colour scheme by being painted, bound with ribbon and decorated with beads or flowers.

● Above: *Decorating a candlestick with crystal drops will give it a dressed-up evening look. It does not matter if the drops do not all match, as that only makes the overall effect more interesting. These drops have been wired into position using fine florist's wire.*

● Right: *A firm favourite with Scandinavians, candle rings can be made from flowers, foliage or even papercuts. This is an easy way to give the table a seasonal feel or to adapt candlesticks to alternative schemes. These pretty variegated euphorbia leaves create a fresh feel with glass candlesticks. A note of caution: blow out the candle before it burns down to the level of the candle ring.*

● Right: *Pretty floating flower candles can be enhanced by the real thing in a glass tazza. For a small container like this one, choose tiny flowers to provide a contrast with the wax version. Alternatively, you could use a large bowl with several floating candles set off by larger real flowers, such as colourful gerberas.*

● Left: *One, two or three leaf-wrapped candles can be positioned in the centre of the table, or at each guest's place. Wrapping candles in artichoke leaves is particularly appropriate for a meal where artichokes are being served: you can take outer leaves from each head for each candle (choose pillar candles about 9 x 5cm/3½ x 2in). Tie on the leaves using a narrow piece of raffia, and set each candle on a small plate decorated with ornamental cabbage leaves or any other pretty foliage.*

DECORATIONS

Table decorations are the most CREATIVE ELEMENT of table settings. They are not grounded to the practicalities of the designs of the tableware you happen to own, and they can be – indeed, they often have to be – different every time you entertain. This is because table decorations are often organic: for instance, flowers and fruit that CHANGE WITH THE SEASONS.

This is not to say that all decorations have to be ORGANIC: you can use favourite china or glass ornaments, or you can wrap or present PARTY FAVOURS in any number of ways, adding to the decorative element of the table. Even though table decorations are normally associated with one large TABLE CENTREPIECE, you do not have to be limited to this. Very often it is easier to decorate crowded tables with smaller arrangements at each setting. These take up less space and add a much more personal touch.

● Right: *Fresh flowers are still the favourite ingredient for table decorations, giving a delightful seasonal feel to the setting.*

DECORATION DIRECTORY

As with the rest of the home, almost anything can become a decoration and, indeed, you may even want to use favourite ornaments as a finishing touch to the table. Traditionally, however, table centrepieces are often floral, lending a seasonal feel to the setting. Food, too, can be used decoratively – most usually in the form of fruits or sweets, which are brought on after the main course. Other forms of decoration include place names and party favours. However you wish to decorate the table, there are two restrictions. The most obvious is the space on the table. Few of us are lucky enough to have huge tables, and very often the place settings and the food itself take up most of the space. The second consideration is the eye level of the diners. A tall, dense arrangement that interferes with cross-table conversation will not aid the conviviality of the party.

Flower arrangements do not necessarily require grand containers. A simple plate with a low arrangement fixed into florist's foam, for example, can be stunning. Or the more decorative jam jars, perhaps tied with string, raffia or ribbon, can look terrific. You may like to create a little height, using an urn, tazza or cake stand for fruit or floral arrangements. Varying the height on the table does give the whole table setting depth, but you must keep everything below eye level.

Party favours are another opportunity for table decoration. These are usually some kind of sweets, often done up in muslin pouches the Continental way. There is no reason, however, why they should not be wrapped in cellophane instead and then arranged in miniature baskets, or placed inside pretty fabric drawstring bags.

● Above: *Topiary trees have an architectural quality that gives a smart edge to any table. Stand one at each place setting, or let several march down the length of the table.*

● Right: *Frosted fruit can be arranged in an elegant tazza to become an exquisite table decoration. At the end of the meal, everyone can partake.*

● Above: *Place names can be embellished with a bow. Wire-edged gold organza ribbon makes a simple place card very special.*

● Right: *Almost anything can be turned into a table decoration. A miniature pineapple, for example, wrapped in cellophane and tied with sash cord, looks delightful. Stand a trio of them down the centre of the table.*

● Below: *All sorts of foods look good on the table, even if they are only for decoration. This pile of assorted mushrooms on a pewter plate has an evocative French farmhouse feel.*

● Above: *Bunches of herbs and spices can make aromatic decorations. Here, a bunch of chilli peppers has simply been placed on a rough-hewn, country-style stone plate.*

DECORATIVE IDEAS

A table decoration can be as simple as a few seasonal flowers in a vase or it can be as elaborate as a formal urn arrangement. But the real creativity comes when you add your own flair, perhaps transcending the obvious. Vases can be wrapped in almost anything from brown paper to string to give myriad new looks. Flowers can be placed in vases, ready-tied to give them natural-looking support; if the container is glass, the securing string will add to the decoration. Flowers, foliage and berries can be gilded, and a range of fruits or vegetables added to a floral arrangement. Flowers with straight, sturdy stalks, such as tulips or daffodils, can be stood on plates or in shallow bowls, tied to keep them in an upright position.

Fruits and vegetables make wonderful organic table arrangements. As well as the more obvious grapes, pears, figs and pomegranates, you can use pumpkins and squashes, perhaps decoratively carved and internally lit with a night-light. Gilding fruits and vegetables, or tying them up with string or raffia, adds the extra touch to make them different.

Party favours can be extremely decorative. They could consist of a few sweets – gold or silver dragées or foil-wrapped truffles – or a small gift wrapped in muslin, brocade, cellophane or paper. Use these like accessories to complement the colour scheme, just as jewellery complements an outfit.

● Above: *Bound with green raffia and placed upright in a shallow glass bowl, a bunch of asparagus makes a witty display. Use this arrangement either purely decoratively, or as a starter, supplying scissors for guests to snip off the raffia before eating.*

● Above: *Given extra touches, even an old jam jar can take on an enchanting appearance. Here, cotton string adds to the appeal of an antique French jar, but the idea will work just as well with attractive modern jars. The key is not to overdo it. Keep to simple additions when the container itself is simple, and then the flowers inside it will shine.*

● Above: *When the sweets used for party favours – such as these dragées and crystallized violets – are visually pleasing in themselves, show them off in cellophane and lay them on a co-ordinating plate. Cut a square of cellophane, bring two adjacent sides together to make a cone and fix with adhesive tape. Fill the cone with sweets, then tie with broad ribbon and trim the ends.*

● Above: *Place decorations are extra-special when they are scented. These highly perfumed narcissi would make wonderful treats for dinner guests. Provide additional visual interest by potting them in clay pots, adding contorted willow branches and tying them with fine cotton string.*

FURNITURE

Furniture, the single most expensive component of table settings, provides the very bones of dining. It can be used to MAKE A STATEMENT and to set the style to which everything else conforms, or it can take the supporting role. If you buy a dining suite, you are likely to keep it for a very long time, so choose a CLASSIC STYLE that will not date. But the most important factor in the choice is

COMFORT. Sharing meals is one of the most sociable of our activities, and one when we all want to feel our MOST RELAXED. Unless you have a lot of space and a large table, consider also the widths of the chairs: unnecessarily wide seats can lead to a cramped feeling. An incongruous table can be covered with a cloth. Even if you have the most EXQUISITE TABLE, by sometimes adding cloths or different table mats you can create a wide variety of different looks from one set of furniture.

● Right: *Choose chairs to complement the style of your dining room, while relating their proportions to the dining table.*

FURNITURE FILE

The sculptural lines of tables and chairs lend themselves to many materials: metal, wood, upholstery, rush and cane. And for each one there are endless styles and finishes. Your own personal choice will be limited by the size of your dining room or eating area and the style of the rest of your home. If it has a cottagey look, you may prefer country furniture for the dining room, choosing wooden kitchen-style chairs; alternatively, you may prefer the look of Mediterranean taverna chairs with rush seats and painted frames. Cottage- or farmhouse-style tables may be in simple stripped pine, or limed or painted.

More formal, traditional dining rooms are likely to be furnished with highly polished tables and chairs, or Louis XV French-style furniture. Modern, formal dining furniture includes clean-lined glass, metal or fine wood. Less formal family homes may use garden chairs doubled up for indoor dining use, or they may bring out reinforcement folding chairs when guest numbers increase.

While folding chairs have been generally considered to have a utilitarian appearance, the pressure of space in many modern homes has encouraged a number of designers to put their best efforts into creating these versatile pieces of furniture. The Italians, particularly, have produced some exquisite modern designs that combine essential space-saving requirements with an indisputably elegant form.

● Left: *Folding garden chairs can double up as indoor dining chairs. This type of traditional English design was often used by cricket spectators who needed a seat intended to offer comfort for most of the day.*

● Right: *The straight and parallel form of this chair gives away its modern design. The rush seat typifies its Mediterranean country roots, as seen in the classic Greek taverna chair.*

● Above: *French-style dining chairs combine elegance with comfort. Their generously upholstered seats bear witness to the French love of sharing good food at ease over long periods of time. The graceful curves of the legs keep the overall design light.*

● Above: *Traditional farmhouse kitchen chairs lend a homely feel.*

● Above: *Modern styles often have simple, uncluttered lines, as seen in this chair with a metal frame "upholstered" with woven natural cane.*

● Right: *Metal French-style parlour chairs have recently enjoyed a renaissance. They have a wonderfully graceful look, their finely detailed backs lending a light, airy feel to the whole dining area.*

FURNITURE FINISHES

Several years ago, there was a fashion for completely bandaging dining chairs, Egyptian-mummy style, wrapping them in fabric, or making tailored slip-over covers. Most of us today would consider this a time-consuming performance with very little reward when you consider that, once the guests are seated, not much of the chair is on show. Perhaps much better would be to cover just the tops of the chair backs, or to add a thoughtful touch to delight guests as they come to the table and while they are getting comfortable. A small gift on each seat, a scented bouquet tied to the back, or eye-catching tassels all provide extra detail for special celebrations. Another, rather more practical, idea where space is tight is to tie place cards to the backs of the chairs, freeing the table top of clutter. Decorating chair backs can also be an opportunity to tie in the colours of the rest of the table setting.

For tables, the obvious finishing touch is to add a tablecloth, which can be done with flair for effect. You may wish to give a different look to a beautifully finished table, yet not want to shroud it in a cloth. In this situation try using a translucent fabric such as muslin, tulle or organza to veil the table without obscuring it. This effect could be taken a step further by placing a decorative item on the table top to show through the cloth. Leaves, flowers, feathers, ribbons or bows can each give a completely different feel to the same setting.

● Above: *Hanging place cards from the backs of the dining chairs frees table space for the more important matter of eating. This example was cut from decorated parchment notepaper and tied with a co-ordinating golden cord.*

● Right: *Tassels tied to each chair give them an elegant dressed-for-the-occasion look. Tassels and cord in a range of colours are sold in the haberdashery departments of most large stores.*

● Above: *A herbal posy tied to each chair back looks delightful and releases an inimitable aroma as people brush past, exciting the taste buds even before the meal has properly got underway. Alternatively, small bunches of dried flowers in colours to match the table decoration would be just as attractive, although less fragrant.*

● Left: *Party favours on seats have treasure-hunt appeal: they are so unexpected and the surprise is only revealed once the chairs are pulled out. They look wonderful when co-ordinated with the tones of the chairs themselves. This pretty example consists of an oval gift box wrapped loosely in gold organza; this has been secured with a textured gold ribbon for maximum impact.*

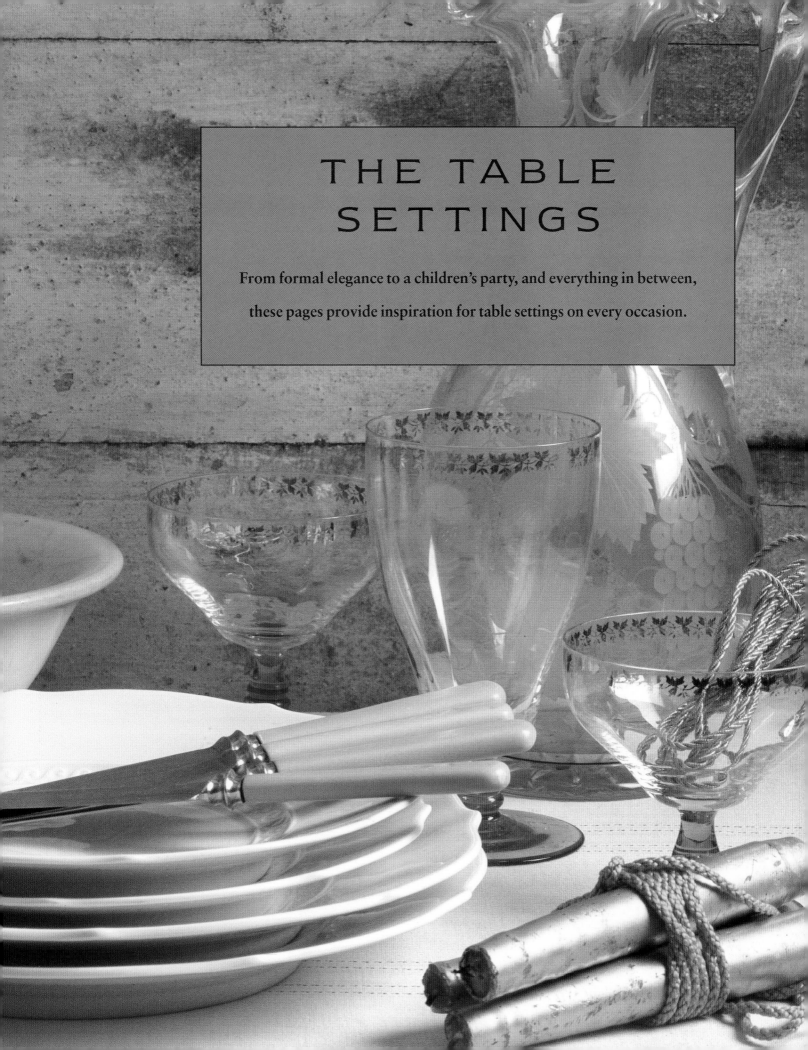

THE TABLE SETTINGS

From formal elegance to a children's party, and everything in between,
these pages provide inspiration for table settings on every occasion.

LAYING THE TABLE WITH FLAIR

While the first part of the book discussed inspirational ideas on choosing and using all the elements of table settings, the following pages show how to put them all together.

Although etiquette dictates how and where everything should be put on the table for formal occasions, nowadays this is becoming less rigid. As long as everything is arranged so that the progress of the meal or the conversation is not interfered with, and as long as everyone is comfortable, then modern etiquette should be satisfied. Happily, this loosening of formality opens the doors to much more creative treatment of the table for entertaining.

The table settings shown in the following pages are designed to inspire, providing ideas for the use of colour and pattern as well as suggesting creative ways to add extra flair to the various elements. They can all be adapted to tables for as many or as few guests as you wish to invite, and the ideas can be used for setting a buffet table as well as for sit-down meals.

The main difference between buffet tables and those laid out with place settings is that the conversation does not have to be carried out across them. This means that floral arrangements and candles can be taller, possibly making a greater statement. Also, china can be – and indeed, will probably have to be – stacked higher and cutlery piled up or placed in a container.

The use of colour can have a huge impact on the table setting, allowing a single dinner service to be adapted in a number of different ways. Coloured tablecloths and linens can be brought

● Above: *Set on a white china tazza, fresh figs with their exquisite purple bloom make a beguiling centrepiece. The use of unusual or organic decorations such as these, especially if set at a higher level than the other table decorations, will create an eye-catching display.*

● Left: *Decorative starters, laid out before the diners are asked to be seated, add to the richly textured quality of the table setting. Here, artichokes are served on amber glass plates laid on brass underplates, and are topped by skeletonized magnolia leaves.*

into play, and the tones of these can be complemented by floral and other table decorations. You can also add colour by using underplates, or by placing decorative and colourful starters on the plates before inviting diners to take their places.

Whatever the style or colour of the table setting, the use of varying heights will always create interest. Stacked plates and bowls – each place setting may consist of an underplate, a dinner plate and a soup plate, for example – offer more dimension than a single flat plate. You may then have low serving dishes teamed with taller tureens, cake stands, tazzas or even urns for flowers. Candles and their holders offer plenty of scope for varying levels. Some can be low, bringing light at table - top level; others may be raised higher on candlesticks or in candle holders. While some height is desirable, it should never be brought above the eye level of the diners, as this would greatly interfere with the conversation.

The table settings illustrated in this section of the book show just a few of the many possibilities. Try out and adapt the ideas yourself, using the elements of tableware you already have. Alternatively, add some new finds and ideas to create your own, individual table-setting flair.

● Above: *A pair of delicate porcelain cherubs, along with an elegant place card, mark the bride's place at a wedding banquet. Visually appealing touches like this will make the difference between an ordinary table setting and a really memorable one.*

● Left: *When the colours are right, and when there is a generous mix of styles, you can happily combine modern translucent acrylic-stemmed cutlery with elegant antique silver pieces.*

WHITE MAGIC

Translucent CRUNCHY ORGANDIE gives a crisp and airy look to this most elegant of table settings. The GRACEFULLY CURVED shapes of the china and glass are contrasted against the similar curves of a pewter dish and jugs. The WHITE AMARYLLIS blooms set into one of the jugs

form a dramatic floral centrepiece for the table, yet could not be easier to put in place. The curves and points of their spectacular petals echo the FLOWING LINES of the plate edgings. Delicate detailing throughout is set against the smooth lines of the main pieces. The glasses and decanter are decorated with TRACERY LINES in white, then given sparkle with diamanté. Napkins are tied with white GAUZY RIBBON, and the final touch is provided by organdie party favours tied with diamanté-decorated ribbons for guests to take home as souvenirs.

● Right: *Painted glasses and organdie sachets filled with pot-pourri perfectly complement pure white and pewter.*

PAINTED GLASSES

Decorated glasses add a special touch to a celebration table setting. Hand-painted with white matt emulsion, the patterns will wash off; for a more permanent pattern, use glass paint. If you are less than confident about painting freehand, draw out the pattern on a piece of paper first, then slip this inside the glass and paint over the lines.

MATERIALS

- stemmed glasses
- white matt emulsion or glass paint
- small artist's brush
- tweezers
- all-purpose glue
- diamanté stones

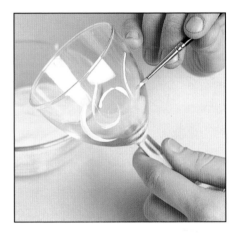

1 Holding the glass by the stem, paint on sweeping lines and curves using the artist's brush. Allow to dry.

2 Use the tweezers to dab a little glue on to the back of each diamanté stone laid face down on a fingertip. Carefully press into position on the glass.

POT-POURRI SACHETS

These sachets will scent the air during the meal and make welcome party favours to take home.

MATERIALS

- organdie
- pinking shears
- pot-pourri
- fine wire
- rayon ribbon
- diamanté stones
- all-purpose glue

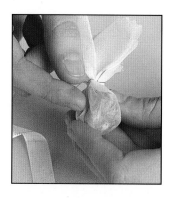

1 Cut a circle of organdie, and then fill the centre with pot-pourri. Draw the organdie together around the filling.

2 Wind fine wire around the sachet to secure it. Tie on a length of ribbon and glue on some diamanté stones.

● Above: *Delicate organdie napkins are tied with gauzy white ribbon and trimmed with a chandelier drop.*

● Above: *Fine bone china in purest white always looks elegant, even if the pieces do not match.*

CITRUS
SHADES

The wonderful clear tones of citrus fruits are hard to resist, evoking TANGY FRESHNESS and hot Mediterranean days. Though these fruits are often associated with clean-toned plastics and crisp (if not hard-edged) schemes, they can be used in a more

EARTHY way, too. The scheme shown here has been kept to fresh lemons and limes, while the WARM TONES of terra-cotta pots are used to represent oranges. The fruits are used in a decorative way throughout the table setting: in an urn as a STRIKING CENTREPIECE, individually in small pots as place-setting decorations, and hollowed out to hold candles. The colours are linked with the lemon-yellow napkins, which have been given a simple appliqué edging in lime. The theme is pursued in the LIME-COLOURED china and glass and in the fresh green leaves .

● Right: *The sharp tones of lemons and limes take on a richer look when teamed with earthy terracotta and rusty iron.*

DECORATED FRUITS

These lemon skins have been given a chequered look using a lemon zester. The technique could just as easily be carried out on limes or even oranges – or a combination of all three.

MATERIALS

- lemons
- lemon zester

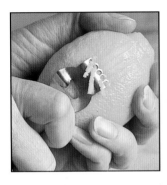

1 Use the zester to cut vertical lines, dividing the lemon into quarters. Next, make two rows of horizontal lines in each quarter: vary the spacing between the rows on different lemons, for added interest.

● Left: *Lemons in old terracotta pots encircled with narrow paper ribbon make enchanting place decorations. If you have larger pots, you could fill them with different fruits such as pineapples or watermelons. If possible, use pots that have an attractive "weathered" look for a greater sense of texture. If you do not have such pots at home, you may well be able to buy them cheaply from a garden centre.*

CITRUS CENTREPIECE

Lemons and limes piled high in an urn have a distinctly Mediterranean look. A rusted metal urn gives the centrepiece a wonderfully earthy feel, but you could use any shallow, wide-necked container. The lemons and limes have been bound together with florist's wire to keep them in place.

MATERIALS

- urn
- bubble wrap to fit inside the urn, or other filling material
- lemons
- limes
- lemon zester
- florist's medium-gauge stub wires
- wire cutters

1 Fill the urn with bubble wrap or filling and cover this with a layer of lemons and limes. Carve one or two lemons with the zester (as opposite, above) if desired.

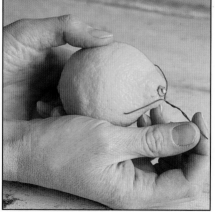

2 Push a short piece of stub wire through one end of each lemon and lime, then twist the ends together.

3 Pile up the fruits, supporting each one by pushing the wires into a fruit below.

LIME CANDLES

Enchanting lime candles are not difficult to make and do not require any special equipment. Use melted church candles because they have long burn times, which is important because limes are small. Place each lime candle on a saucer.

MATERIALS

- limes
- small paring knife
- teaspoon
- church candles
- scissors
- double boiler
- small saucers

1 Cut the top off each lime and shave off the bottom so that they stand straight. Use a teaspoon to scoop out the contents.

2 Break up the candles and slip them off their wicks. Cut the wicks to size. Slowly melt the candles in a double boiler.

3 Pour a little wax into the bottom of each lime skin and insert the wicks. Using a warmed teaspoon, fill up the lime skins with wax. Place on the saucers.

APPLIQUÉ NAPKINS

Appliqué does not have to be intricate, complex or time-consuming. Even the simplest design, trimming the ends of a napkin, can give it a more finished look. Use ready-made napkins, or make them yourself from 30 x 30cm/12 x 12in squares of fabric.

MATERIALS

- lime-coloured napkin
- scissors
- paper
- iron
- ironing board
- needle
- matching thread
- 6 lemon-coloured napkins

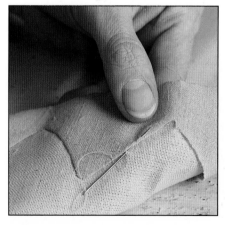

1 Cut a 5cm/2in wide strip off one side of the lime napkin and fold it in half crossways, in half again and in half a third time. Cut a piece of paper to this width, and then fold it in half and snip off one corner. Open out the paper and use it as a template to cut the corners of the folded lime strip. Open out the zigzag edging.

2 Fold over a 1cm/¼in hem along the full length of the lime strip and along the short ends. Using a hot iron, press the hem into position. Neatly slip-stitch the straight edge of the lime strip to the edge of the lemon napkin.

3 Slip-stitch the zigzag edge of the strip to the napkin, turning in the edges as you go. You will only need to turn in these edges very slightly – just enough to neaten them – or you may find it difficult to create the "points" at the inner and outer corners of the zigzag.

CHINA
BLUES

Blue and white are classic colours for china, reminiscent of OLD CHINESE DESIGNS and traditional English patterns. Blues on blues make a wonderful mix. You can either keep to LAVENDER blues, lean towards greener denim blues, or mix them all together. If you want to use SEVERAL BLUES, mix at least three

and you will achieve a very pleasing overall effect. White mixed with blue looks both fresh and clean, and this combination is readily available in a multitude of inexpensive containers and cloths. Simple chambray, ginghams and tea towels can easily be given an elegant finishing touch with the addition of fringing and tassels. Dried lavender is the ideal material for an everlasting table decoration to go with the blues. Here, lavender has been used to create a charming topiary tree, which is surprisingly easy to make.

● Right: *Blue and white make a fresh combination that works well both for a traditional look and for this modern feel.*

CHENILLE NAPKIN TASSELS

Chenille tassels add a glamorous finishing touch to napkins and tablecloths. They are easy to make, and there is a wide choice of colours in chenille knitting yarns.

MATERIALS
- ball of chenille knitting yarn
- scissors
- darning needle
- napkins

1 Make a 15cm/6in skein of chenille to half the desired thickness of the finished tassel. Cut a separate short length of chenille.

2 Fold the skein over the short length of chenille (this will be used to sew the tassel to the napkin). Cut another length of chenille.

3 Wind this second piece of chenille around the top of the skein and secure the end. Trim the bottom of the tassel. Use the "hanging" yarn to sew the tassel to the corner of the napkin.

LAVENDER TOPIARY TREES

These charming, twiggy lavender trees are both a visual delight and a source of that distinctive aroma experienced on hot summer days in Provence.

MATERIALS

- scissors
- florist's foam ball or cone, to fit bowl
- small bowl
- lavender fabric to cover bowl
- glue gun and hot-wax glue sticks
- 4 bunches of dried lavender
- 2 x 5cm/2in florist's foam balls
- large branch of contorted willow
- secateurs
- handful of reindeer moss
- wire cutters
- 2 florist's medium-gauge stub wires, or garden wire

1 Cut the florist's foam ball or cone to fit the bowl. Wrap the fabric around the bowl, tucking in the corners and raw edges. Use spots of hot glue to fix it in place. Put the foam into the bowl and glue in place.

2 Cut the lavender stalks to within 2.5cm/1in of the heads. Fix a circle of heads around the circumference of one of the 5cm/2in foam balls. Make another circle at right angles to the first so that the ball is divided into quarters. Fill in the quarters with lavender. Repeat with the other ball.

3 Cut two "trunks" from the contorted willow, reserving any finer twiggy bits for decoration. Push the "trunks" and twiggy pieces into the foam in the bowl. Glue a lavender ball to the top of each trunk. "Plant" the twiggy pieces of willow into the foam in the bowl. Fix moss to the foam using short lengths of bent wire.

73

THE MIDAS TOUCH

Add a little gold to anything and it becomes very special indeed, but pile it on too enthusiastically and it can be overpowering. The best solution is to MIX THE METALS, using brass, pewter and even tarnished silver. If your crockery cupboard does not stretch to all these materials, try a length of GOLD ORGANZA

trimmed with gold furnishing braid as an overcloth. Gold-rimmed glasses and remnant brocade made into napkins are two inexpensive ways to add JUST ENOUGH GLITZ. Take a tip from gilders of old, who used to apply gold leaf over a base of ox-blood red, deep turquoise or ochre. Here, the scheme is based on turquoise with a silk sari providing the undercloth. Use picture framer's gilt wax to ADD A GLINT to flower arrangements, or pears, for a dramatic golden centrepiece.

● Right: *Glowing candlelight brings out the opulent warmth and golden colours of this festive table setting.*

● Above: *Remnant furnishing brocade, cut into napkin-sized pieces and then hemmed on all sides, becomes rich table linen, especially when tied with two tones of velvet ribbon.*

● Right: *By rubbing on a little picture framer's gilt wax, it is easy to turn everyday items into very special decorations. Here, ordinary William pears have been rubbed with gold, then set in a silver cake stand to become spectacular table ornaments. One pear has been left ungilded to add some organic texture and to prevent the arrangement from becoming too opulent.*

GOLD-RICH TABLE LINEN

Gold metal-shot organza is not expensive and, used as an overcloth, you do not need a large amount. It immediately brings the gold touch to any setting, looking especially rich when used over slubbed silk or a sari, as here.

MATERIALS

- gold metal-shot organza, to cover the table and slightly overlap the sides
- needle
- thread
- scissors
- gold furnishing braid to trim all the edges, plus an additional 15cm/6in for the corners

1 Make a hem along all edges of the organza, then slip-stitch the braid in place, making a loop at each corner.

GILDED LILY CENTREPIECE

When yellow flowers somehow do not seem rich enough for a gold scheme, take rust-coloured ones and add your own golden touch. This low copper and silver bowl of rust-coloured calla lilies and tree ivy provides an easy-to-make yet exotically golden centrepiece for a table.

MATERIALS

- scissors
- florist's foam
- shallow metal bowl
- picture framer's gilt wax
- 12 calla lilies
- small bunch of tree ivy, with berries

1 Cut the florist's foam to fit the bowl, then soak it in water. Use the picture framer's gilt wax to gild all the lilies. Cut the stems to just a few centimetres long, then fix them into the florist's foam so that they all face outwards.

2 Gild the tree ivy – both the leaves and the berries – with picture framer's gilt wax. Use the ivy to fill the gaps in the arrangement, pushing each sprig firmly into the foam.

JEWEL BRIGHTS

Take inspiration from India, the home of sapphires and rubies, turquoise and lapis lazuli, to create a RICH JEWELLED look. Gather together simple ingredients in these glorious shades from high street shops, to create a feel that is ROMANTIC AND EXOTIC.

There is an abundance of Middle Eastern COLOURED GLASS crockery – choose the frosted kind like this, or the simple rustic blown sort that is thick with bubbles. The rich colours are EASY TO MIX in both crockery and linens. Here, vivid sapphire crockery and table linens are ENRICHED with turquoise and a touch of ruby in the form of exotic fruits and flowers. Emerald greens could work just as well mixed with the blues and rubies. To emphasize the jewelled look, a BEADED FRINGE has been added to the tablecloth.

● Right: *Use coloured-glass beads to lend an exotic touch to jewel-toned linen and matching crockery.*

● Right: *An old birdcage makes a witty candle holder that becomes a focal point for the table. The candles are fixed into a toning blue-enamelled brass bowl from India using some hot wax, then lit and carefully placed in the birdcage. This type of old-fashioned cage is now a popular item for home decoration, but the cages can still sometimes be bought very cheaply from junk shops.*

BEADED TABLECLOTH FRINGE

The beads are sewn on to the tablecloth at 7.5cm/3in intervals, so measure the hem to find out how many "tassels" you will need. To wash the cloth, slip it into a pillowcase first to prevent the beads from damaging the inside of the machine.

MATERIALS

- scissors
- button thread
- long, fine needle
- frosted glass beads
- small metallized plastic beads in 2 different shapes
- small glass beads
- tablecloth large enough to hang down from the table

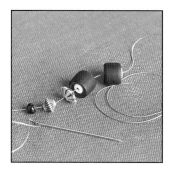

1 Cut a length of button thread and thread on two frosted glass beads, two metallized plastic beads and one small glass bead.

2 Take the thread around the outside of the small glass bead, then pass the needle back through all the other beads. Re-thread the needle with both ends of thread and sew firmly to the tablecloth.

BEAD NAPKIN RINGS

This elaborate-looking style of napkin ring is very easy to make. You need small beads for the sides and larger ones for the "rungs", but it does not matter if they do not match. A rich variation of beads makes the finished effect more attractive.

MATERIALS

- scissors
- button thread
- 2 long, fine needles
- large glass beads of approximately the same length, but varying in width and design
- smaller glass beads, in 2 contrasting colours and slightly different sizes

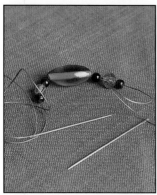

1 Cut a length of button thread and thread a needle on to each end. Thread on one large bead. Next, thread three smaller beads on either side of the large bead.

2 Thread another large bead on to one side, then pass the other needle through in the opposite direction.

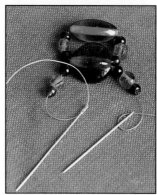

3 Pull both threads taut, then thread three small beads on to each needle.

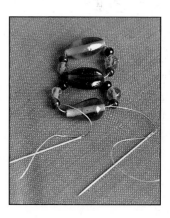

4 Repeat steps 2 and 3 until you have used all the beads. Complete the napkin ring by threading the ends back through the first bead. Tie the ends together securely and trim.

OUT OF
AFRICA

The bold designs and STRONG, EARTHY COLOURS that hail from Africa add up to a dramatic look that is easy to put together. Start with black and cream for printed textiles, china and earthenware, then add TERRACOTTA TONES using garden pots, thick-ribbed burnt-orange cottons and various beans for

decorative use. Trim candle holders and make napkin rings with wooden BEADS AND SEEDS in all the earth shades.

String is an easy and inexpensive way to add pattern, lending texture to table mats. It can also be used for trimming the corners of the tablecloth. An easy way to give a ZIGZAG appearance to the edge of the tablecloth is to lay two or more smaller cloths on the diagonal. Attaching a flamboyant ORANGE STRING BOBBLE to each corner adds a touch of wit to this earthy design.

● Right: *Wooden beads, exotic seeds and string make inexpensive ingredients for an authentic African look.*

● Right: *China in all the earth shades can be freely mixed and matched. Choose plain pieces or those with simple line patterns. If you are lucky you may find two differently patterned sets of china that match well, as shown here. The decorations are very simple but remarkably effective when combined in this way.*

STRING-DECORATED TABLE MATS

Plain modern table mats in strong, earthy colours can be quickly given African appeal by adding a free-form border in string. This is an effective technique and easy to carry out, if you are reasonably handy with a needle and thread.

MATERIALS

- thick-ribbed cotton table mats
- jute string
- scissors
- pins
- needle and thread

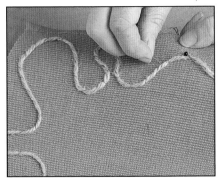

1 Make a squiggly free-form design all around the border of the table mat, pinning the string into position as you go. Sew it in place using small stitches.

STRING BOBBLE TRIMMINGS

Eye-catching orange string balls are easy to make, and look wonderful trimming the sides as well as the corners of tablecloths. Use two small tablecloths for this design, and lay them diagonally over a larger, plain undercloth so that the bobbles hang down the sides.

MATERIALS

- all-purpose or paper glue
- polystyrene craft balls, the size of golf balls
- roll or skein of paper string
- scissors
- needle
- thread
- 2 small tablecloths

1 Apply glue to the bottom of the ball, then wind on the paper string, working round in an even spiral. Once the glued part is covered, add more glue to the uncovered part of the ball and continue winding. When the whole ball is covered with string, make a loop at the top for hanging, neatening this off by tucking the end under the last spiral.

2 Use the needle and thread to stitch the bobble to the corner of the tablecloth.

ETHNIC NAPKIN RINGS

Knotted on to a thong to reveal some of the leather, interestingly shaped beads can be crafted into highly effective napkin rings. Simply wrap the beaded thong loosely around the napkin several times and knot the two ends together.

MATERIALS

For each napkin ring:

- 30cm/12in tanned leather thong
- selection of wooden and seed beads

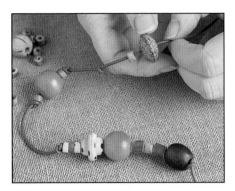

1 Make a knot about 5cm/2in from one end of the thong. Thread on a few beads, then tie another knot. Tie a third knot a short distance from the second knot. Add some more beads, then tie another knot. Continue threading on beads until you reach 5cm/2in from the other end of the thong. Tie the final knot.

DECORATIVE BEAN BALLS

Dried beans and berries are wonderful materials for making decorative balls. Piled together in an old copper bowl, the balls become a wonderful organic table decoration.

MATERIALS

- glue gun and hot-wax glue sticks
- cotton wadding balls
- selection of dried beans and/or berries
- shallow copper bowl

1 Apply hot-wax glue to a small part of a cotton wadding ball, then add the beans or berries. Add more glue, then more beans, and continue in this way until the whole ball is covered.

BEADED CANDLE POTS

Decorated with a garland of beads, an ordinary terracotta garden pot makes a striking and very stable candle holder. The old-fashioned style of pots – stained from years of exposure to the elements – are especially effective, and contribute to the textural, earthy feel of the decoration.

MATERIALS

- florist's medium-gauge wire
- wire cutters
- natural-coloured beads, in a variety of shapes and sizes
- glue gun and hot-wax glue sticks
- terracotta pots
- florist's putty, or a piece of crock or stone
- sand
- trowel
- candles

1 Wrap the wire twice around the first bead, and twist in the end to secure. Thread on the rest of the beads.

2 Use the glue gun to attach the garland of beads at intervals around the rim of the pot.

3 Stop up the drainage hole with florist's putty, or with a piece of crock or stone.

4 Fill the pot with sand and then stand the candles in the sand, pushing them in far enough to be well supported.

BEACH STYLE

The neutral tones and BEGUILING FORMS found on the beach provide wonderful inspiration for table decoration. The SILVERY GREYS and soft beiges of pebbles, driftwood and old galvanized metal teamed with the CORAL PINKS of shells and sea-washed

terracotta create a winning combination. Use them for a table setting at home, or take some complementary colours for a simple SEASIDE PICNIC to eat on the rocks. Inspired by the soft shades of a northern beach in winter rather than the dazzling hues of a summer's day, this setting conjures up the peacefulness of a deserted shore. SIMPLICITY is the key: a few shells sewn to napkins, a sculptural centrepiece of DRIFTWOOD and found features, and a candle pot decorated with seashells. Natural linens, stone, wood and unpolished metal cutlery will complement the subtle toning.

● Right: *Add finishing touches of shell-edged napkins, a sand-dollar candle pot and driftwood sculpture to a seaside setting.*

● Left: *A piece of driftwood accessorized with seabird feathers becomes an evocative centrepiece. If you are picnicking on the beach, make an instant sculpture; at home, put together holiday finds to create an eye-catching design for your table.*

SHELL CANDLE POT

Not only does this beach-inspired candle pot bring natural lighting to the table, but it makes the perfect seaside centrepiece.

MATERIALS

- medium-sized terracotta garden pot, plus a smaller pot to fit inside
- linen muslin, or other natural loose-weave fabric such as scrim
- glue gun and hot-wax glue sticks
- sand dollar
- cotton string
- scissors
- 5cm/2in church candle
- small scallop-type shells

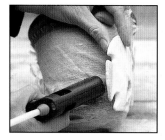

1 Wrap the fabric around the larger pot and glue to fix. Glue the sand dollar to the front of the pot, and then tie it with a cross of string.

2 Put the candle inside the smaller pot and place that inside the larger pot. Decorate the inner rim of the small pot with the scallop-type shells.

SHELL-EDGED NAPKINS

Undyed linen is perfect for beach-style napkins. Buy ready-made napkins or make your own, then trim them with a small shell at each corner, or stitch shells all the way along two opposite sides. The shells will need to have small holes drilled through the tops.

MATERIALS

For each napkin:

- undyed linen, about 30cm/ 12in square
- needle
- matching thread
- cream pearl cotton embroidery thread
- length of fine wire
- 16 shells
- embroidery needle
- scissors

1 Hem all sides of the linen square to make a napkin. Next, thread the embroidery thread through the shells by first making a large knot at one end of a length of doubled thread. Bend the wire in half and thread the looped end down through the shell. Pass the knotted thread through this.

2 Draw the wire back through the shell, pulling the thread with it. The knotted end should stay securely inside the shell. This process can be a little fiddly, and it works better with some shells than others, so try to be patient.

3 Thread the embroidery needle with the doubled end of the embroidery thread and pass the needle through from the back of the napkin, round the back of the thread at the top of the shell, and back through to the back of the napkin.

91

SUN-FILLED STYLE

Evoking HOT, SUNNY DAYS in Greece, Portugal or Provence, this Mediterranean style is simple, country, colourful. The typical palette is CHALKY BLUE and turquoise set against sun-baked terracotta and white. Paint is a favourite medium in that part of the world, and almost everything is given a lick of COLOUR: woodwork,

furniture, tableware and even OLD CANS can be turned into decorative containers. Here, old plates and bowls have been painted and decorated with simple but striking designs for an instant MEDITERRANEAN LOOK. Temporary pattern can be applied with stripes of painted masking tape; napkins and tablecloths can be simply embroidered. For authenticity, scour delicatessens for bright olive-oil cans and use them as highly practical table decorations. Vibrant-coloured flowers add the finishing touch.

● Right: *Bright pastels painted on to plates and table linens, complemented by colourful utensils, add up to Mediterranean style.*

92

● Right: *Olive oil is an ancient symbol of the Mediterranean. Add pretty herbs such as rosemary to complement decorative bottles of oil. All kinds of glass bottles can be used in this way, so never discard your bottles but wash them and keep them to one side. Clear rather than coloured glass – especially when set on a sunny windowsill – will show off the wonderful colours of the oil and herbs.*

EMBROIDERED NAPKINS

Simple straight stitches worked in concentric and starry patterns, and in several bright Mediterranean colours, are a quick way to enliven a set of plain napkins.

MATERIALS

- napkins
- circular object
- pencil
- embroidery needle
- stranded embroidery threads in 3 contrasting colours
- scissors

1 Use a circular object – such as a roll of adhesive tape, as shown here – to draw circles randomly over the whole surface of the napkin.

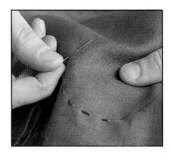

2 Use the drawn circles as a guide to make a spiral of running stitches in the contrasting colours of stranded embroidery thread. Add some six-pointed stars at intervals.

PAINTED WOODEN PLATE

Tatty junk shop finds can be given a new lease of life with brightly coloured paint inspired by the Mediterranean colours. Once protected with a coat of matt varnish, this plate makes an eye-catching underplate, though it is unlikely to withstand the rigours of machine-washing.

MATERIALS

- matt emulsion in 2 contrasting colours
- small decorator's brush
- matt ceramic plate
- masking tape
- small artist's brush
- matt polyurethane varnish
- small brush

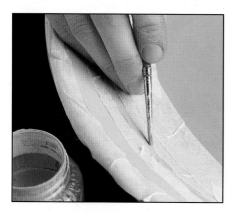

1 Apply an even coat of matt emulsion to the plate and allow to dry. Apply three "stripes" of masking tape around the rim, leaving two exposed ragged lines. Paint these lines with contrasting emulsion, using the fine artist's brush. Allow to dry. Remove the tape and varnish the plate.

STRIPES FOR PLATES

Everyday crockery can be temporarily and quickly transformed using masking tape strips. These can be fixed to the plate in lines or chequered patterns. This technique is ideal for side plates, but is not really suitable for main meal plates.

MATERIALS

- masking tape and card
- matt emulsion
- small artist's brush
- scalpel
- cutting mat
- side plates

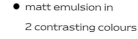

1 Stick masking tape to a piece of card, paint it the colour of your choice, then cut it into fine strips using a scalpel. Peel the tape from the card and stick on to the plates in pairs of parallel lines.

SHAKER
STYLING

Take inspiration from the Shaker style, where patterns are restricted to CHECKS AND STRIPES, and colours are limited to a particular palette ·that includes INDIGO BLUES. Shaker furniture was always made of fine woods, and the designs were clean and unembellished.

This pure simplicity in the use of WOOD furniture is represented here with wooden underplates. A Shaker basket, made from splints of wood rather than the withes (willow twigs) that are more common in Europe, is used as a container for bread. Although the Shakers shunned embellishment for themselves, many craftsmen used the HEART MOTIF on items for sale to represent their maxim: "Hands to work and hearts to God". It can be used, therefore, to decorate the table, appearing on napkins, napkin rings and place decorations.

● Right: *A small topiary tree provides the perfect Shaker decoration on this table – charming but unfussy.*

● Left: *Spare candles, stored in a wooden candle box and decoratively tied around with chequered cloth, can make a charming table decoration. Candles now come in so many different tones that you could fill the holder with coloured candles to match the rest of your table setting, although pure white is perhaps more appropriate to the simple Shaker theme. Candle holders, such as the one shown, are available from candle suppliers, department stores and specialist kitchen shops.*

CROSS-STITCH HEART

It is easy to re-create almost any motif using cross-stitch. Here, this simple technique is used to embroider a Shaker heart on to a set of plain-coloured napkins. Either use ready-made napkins, or take squares of fabric and hem all the edges.

MATERIALS
- pencil and tissue paper
- pins
- napkins
- needle and thread
- scissors

1 Draw out a heart shape in even-sized crosses on the tissue paper. Pin the tissue paper to the napkin, then stitch over the crosses. Make three crosses on each side of the corner of the napkin.

2 Carefully tear away the tissue paper, leaving the stitched design on the napkin. If any small pieces of paper remain caught under the stitches, use the point of the needle to remove them.

PUNCHED-METAL NAPKIN RINGS

Aluminium foil, which is available in rolls from specialist art shops, is strong yet easy to cut and handle. Here, it is transformed into delightful heart-embossed napkin rings. The packaging tube makes a mould for the rings, which are then slipped off the tube and on to napkins.

MATERIALS
- 1m/1yd aluminium foil
- scissors
- packaging tube
- masking tape
- pencil
- paper
- pin
- silver-coloured adhesive tape

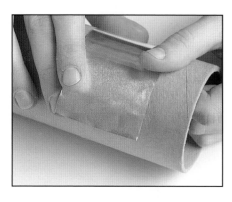

1 Cut a strip of foil about 15 x 5cm/6 x 2in. Wrap this round a packaging tube and secure it with masking tape.

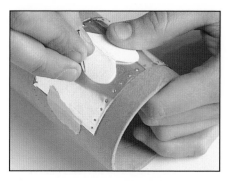

2 Draw and cut out a paper heart about 3.5cm/1½in high. Use a pin to pierce a line of holes along the top and bottom of the foil strip. Place the paper heart centrally on the foil strip and pierce holes around it. Remove the foil from the packaging tube and fold down the top and bottom edges. Join at the back with silver tape.

● Right: *Oval boxes, emblematic of Shaker style, make the perfect packaging for a gift for each guest. Fill them with soap, after-dinner mints or dried herbs.*

WIRE HEARTS

Simple wire hearts make enchanting place decorations. This design is embellished with evergreen leaves to complement the topiary-tree decoration. The heart motif can be used throughout many decorations on the table to effectively capture the essence of Shaker style. These wire hearts are very quick and easy to make, and so they are suitable even for large parties. Make a heart for each of the guests, and then either stand them upright at each place, as shown here, or lay them on the plates – perhaps peeping out from the folds of the napkins.

MATERIALS

For each heart:

- 30cm/12in garden wire
- wire cutters
- 2 small leafy twigs
- fine wire

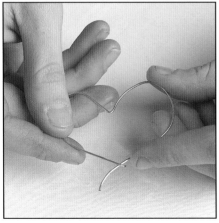

1 Bend the wire into a heart shape, using your fingers to twist the two ends together at the bottom of the heart.

2 Wind one twig on to each side of the wire heart, then bind to the heart at the base with a short length of fine wire. If the twigs do not stay in place, use further lengths of fine wire at intervals to bind them to the heart.

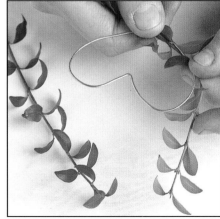

TOPIARY-TREE DECORATION

Topiary trees always make a charming alternative to floral decorations. If you use woody-stemmed evergreen twigs, the tree should last for many days.

MATERIALS

- small florist's foam ball
- evergreen twigs
- secateurs
- small terracotta pot
- florist's foam
- scissors
- straight piece of woody branch
- sphagnum moss
- florist's medium-gauge wire
- wire cutters
- all-purpose glue

1 Soak the florist's foam ball in water. Trim the evergreen twigs to length and push the ends into the florist's foam to provide a lush cover.

2 Soak the remaining florist's foam, cut to fit the pot and place it inside. Push the woody branch down into the centre of the foam so that it is held securely.

3 Cover the florist's foam with moss, and fix it in place with short lengths of florist's wire bent hairpin-style. Fix the leafy ball to the top of the branch and secure it with glue.

MODERN MINIMALISM

The more spare a setting is, the more beautiful each element has to be. FREE OF EMBELLISHMENT, there is no room for rough finishes or incongruous lines. So when planning for this style, study each piece carefully, choosing only ELEGANT DESIGNS that have

a pleasing balance. As different colours and shades have varying effects on the designs, WHITE is a perfect colour choice for a minimalist setting, as it does not detract from the exquisite SHAPES AND FORMS. Here, the white has been broken only by butter-coloured muslin napkins and natural greens. Bamboo-like grasses are used innovatively as mats and napkin rings. The SCULPTED papier-mâché bowl and plate provide exquisite decoration as they await the arrival of WHITE BONE CHINA dinnerware, and the whole effect is supremely elegant.

● Right: *The hand-like forms of a trio of exotic glossy leaves stand out in stark contrast to the pure white of the décor.*

GIANT GRASS MATS

The purpose of a table mat is to protect the furniture from the heat of the plate, but it does not necessarily have to be solid. As long as it holds hot china off the table, then it is perfectly functional. Pliable giant oriental grasses, available from florists, are used here, but you could just as easily use twigs, or even a local sedge or fine bamboo.

MATERIALS

- lengths of oriental grasses
- secateurs or scissors
- garden raffia

1 Cut the grasses to length and form into a triangle with two lengths of grass at the bottom. Bind tightly at each of the places where the grasses cross over, using short lengths of garden raffia.

GIANT GRASS NAPKIN RINGS

These can be made only with pliable material so, if you wish to substitute another material for the grass, try bending it to ensure that it is sufficiently flexible before you begin.

MATERIALS

For each napkin ring:

- about 50cm/20in oriental grasses
- secateurs or scissors
- garden raffia

1 Bend each length of grass into a triangle that is roughly equilateral, leaving the two ends protruding. Bind the grass with garden raffia where the ends cross.

PAPIER-MÂCHÉ PLATE AND BOWL

Formed from recycled paper, papier-mâché is inexpensive, easy to make, and produces surprisingly fine results. The pieces shown here would not be up to serving a whole meal on, but they are a delightfully decorative feature of the table, and could possibly be given as party favours to each guest.

MATERIALS

- plenty of white packing paper
- plate and bowl to use as moulds
- clingfilm
- wallpaper paste
- pastry brush or similar
- white matt emulsion
- small decorator's brush

1 Tear the paper into strips. Cover the plate and bowl with sheets of clingfilm for protection. Make up the wallpaper paste according to the instructions on the packet, and paste the clingfilm using the pastry brush.

2 Lay the paper strips on the clingfilm to cover it, then paste the paper. Apply another layer of paper. Allow to dry thoroughly. Repeat until the desired thickness is reached. Allow to dry thoroughly. This process may take a couple of days, depending on how thick you wish the papier-mâché to be.

3 Very carefully, remove the papier-mâché bowl and plate from their respective moulds, and then paint them with an even coat of white matt emulsion, using the small decorator's brush. Leave the bowl and plate in a safe place to dry thoroughly.

FUN WITH COLOUR

Create the zingiest of table settings by choosing STRONG AND CLASHING COLOURS: fuchsia pink and orange, turquoise blue and yellow. The art is not to be afraid and to throw all the colours in while keeping them close to each other in tone. The feel is FUN, MODERN Continental, with reference to the

FIFTIES' favourite bright pink and turquoise shades in organic free-form shapes. With all this colour, it is wise to keep the setting clean and FREE OF PATTERN. Let ric-rac parcel ties and organic card shapes break solid blocks of colour. Choose gerberas for a floral centrepiece, and place in a brightly coloured enamel jug for an EXUBERANT EFFECT. This is a style in which you can introduce a touch of wit by placing a child's lollipop with each cutlery bundle.

● Right: *Flamboyant colour can be intensified by adding yet more extrovert shades, with flowers and other accessories.*

ZANY GIFTWRAP

Giftwrap does not have to be expensive. Tissue paper and coloured newspaper (search international news stalls for the greatest choice) make perfect wrappings, especially when accessorized by brightly coloured home-made cards and eye-catching ric-rac ties.

MATERIALS

- coloured card
- scissors
- pencil
- hole punch
- scalpel and cutting mat
- gifts
- tissue paper or coloured newspaper
- contrasting ric-rac

1 Cut a gift tag from coloured card. Draw a leaf shape on to the card.

2 Punch a hole in the corner of the card.

3 Cut out most of the design and push it out from the background. Wrap the gift in tissue paper or newspaper and bind with ric-rac. Thread the card on to the ric-rac and tie to secure.

FELT-DECORATED NAPKINS

Appliqué does not necessarily require fiddly and fine needlework. Using simple felt shapes, it can be very quick and easy. These spots and the felt fern shape were stuck on using fabric glue. If you prefer, secure each dot with a tiny stitch and the fern with a stitch at each point.

MATERIALS

- felt
- hole punch
- pencil
- paper
- scissors
- napkins in pink and turquoise
- fabric glue

1 Punch holes in the felt to make dots. Draw the fern shape on paper, cut out and use as a pattern to cut out from felt. Stick the felt fern and dots in position on the napkins using fabric glue.

● Right: *Each place setting features the main colours of fuchsia pink and turquoise.*

● Below: *Make place cards by cutting organic free-form shapes from coloured card using a scalpel. Write on each guest's initial in brightly coloured ink.*

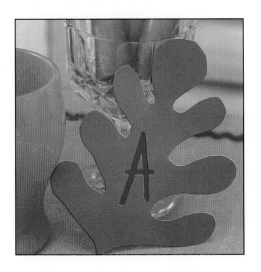

SIMPLY NATURAL

Beautiful table settings are easy to create when you keep everything NATURAL. Leaves and fibres, clays and woods that are happy together outdoors will be happy together indoors, too. Here, the table is covered with HESSIAN – a robust version for the tablecloth, a finer,

paler one to give the place mats greater definition. The FRINGED EDGES, which are easy to do, lend a soft finish, and lines of beads add a pretty touch.

LARGE DRIED LEAVES pinned together with tiny lengths of wood make wonderful alternative place mats. Raffia is used to trim the napkins. Terracotta vases, and earthenware and stone crockery, represent the EARTHY SHADES. Gold initials written on autumn leaves make innovative place names, while chocolate leaves add a delightful ORGANIC-INSPIRED accompaniment for a fruit dessert such as lychees.

● Right: *Let nature dictate the colour scheme using wood, natural undyed fibres and terracotta.*

● Right: *Earthenware and stone plates can be mixed and matched to great effect in natural schemes. The rugged quality of these pieces, with their wonderful texture, would be perfect for a picnic or outdoor table setting.*

LEAF PLACE MATS

You will need strong, slightly flexible dried leaves (available through dried flower specialists) to make these wonderful organic place mats. They are joined together with tiny "pins" of wood, inspired by those used in the southern seas.

MATERIALS
● dried leaves
● small wood stems, cut into 1.5cm/½in lengths

1 Work out the design by laying the leaves down on a flat surface, letting them overlap generously. You can make a circular mat by laying them in concentric circles. Fix the leaves together with the wooden "pins", cut from dried stems. Use about four wooden pins for each leaf, for a firm finish.

CHOCOLATE LEAVES

Leaves made from real chocolate are pretty and impressive garnishes for sweets and puddings. Silk leaves provide the best moulds as they leave a clear impression and will not break up in the chocolate as real leaves can do.

MATERIALS

- high-quality chocolate
- bowl
- saucepan
- silk leaves in a selection of shapes

1 Slowly melt the chocolate in a bowl set over a pan of boiling water. Draw each leaf lightly over the melted chocolate to coat one side and leave on a plate in the freezer to set.

2 When the chocolate is firmly set, carefully peel the silk leaf away. Keep the chocolate leaves in the freezer until you are ready to serve them.

● Left: *Wood-handled cutlery is in keeping with the natural theme. Horn would make a suitable alternative.*

● Below: *Autumn leaves become place cards when each is inscribed with the golden initials of a guest.*

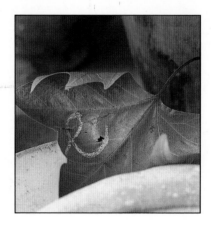

RAFFIA TASSELS

Raffia, which is made from a variety of palm tree, is a wonderful organic material that ties well and withstands washing. It is easy to make up into tasselled napkin rings, that are perfect for this natural look.

MATERIALS

- raffia
- scissors

1 Make a skein of raffia about half the thickness and double the required length of the finished tassel. Tie a few strands of raffia tightly around the centre of the skein, leaving long ends.

2 Fold the skein in half and tie a single piece of raffia near the top of the tassel. Trim the ends of the tassel.

3 Divide the long ends into three, plait them and tie the plait around the napkin.

HESSIAN TABLECLOTH

Made of jute, hessian is a completely natural material that is inexpensive to buy and readily available. A frayed fringe edging and decorative raffia tassels turn what is basically sacking into a smart tablecloth for a range of occasions.

MATERIALS

- hessian to cover the table and hang down at all sides
- scissors
- string
- tapestry needle

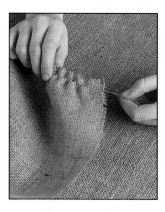

1 Give the cloth straight sides by pulling out a thread from each edge and then cutting very carefully along the space that it leaves.

2 Pull out more threads until the fringing is the desired depth. Sew short lengths of string at intervals into the body of the cloth and then tie into decorative knots.

HESSIAN PLACE MATS

Beads threaded on to string add a decorative detail to place mats that co-ordinate with the tablecloth.

MATERIALS

For each mat:
- fine pale hessian, about 38 x 30cm/15 x 12in
- scissors
- 6 wooden beads
- fine jute string
- tapestry needle

1 Fray the edges of the mat as for the tablecloth. Thread three wooden beads on to a length of string, making a knot around each bead to hold it firmly. Repeat with a second length of string, then stitch the strings in place at each side of the mat.

115

OUTDOOR PARTY

Much of the joy of entertaining outdoors is the impromptu feel of the occasion: the gathering together of what is IN SEASON and allowing that to govern the colours. An abundant bunch of MERRY MARIGOLDS, iris leaves for weaving into table mats and tree ivy for arranging as mats are the starting point for the colour

scheme chosen here. It has been freshened up with clear blue table linen, candlesticks and china. The use of several colours also helps when catering for LARGE PARTIES as it allows several different sets of china to be mixed and matched. Toning green lanterns hang from an overhead branch to lend a soft, FLATTERING LIGHT that is supplemented by the candles on the table itself. The buffet-table theme has been wittily extended to an OLD BIRDCAGE hanging on the the wall.

● Right: *Seasonal leaves and flowers make fun decorations and table mats for an outdoor party setting.*

● Left: *A disused birdcage, containing flowers and a candle in a glass holder, provides a wall-hung montage to complement the table setting.*

● Above: *Carefully arranged green leaves, held together at the centre with a pin, can be used as decorative mats for candles or glasses.*

HANGING LANTERNS

Lanterns are a good solution for outdoor lighting, as they can survive a breeze that would quickly snuff out a candle. You can make hanging lanterns from any glass tumblers or jars with a lip that would support a wire or cord for hanging.

MATERIALS

- green twine
- lipped glass tumblers or jars
- scissors
- garden wire
- wire cutters
- night-lights or small candles

1 Tie some green twine snugly around the lip of each tumbler or jar, and twist a length of garden wire around the twine to make a hanging wire. Place the night-lights or candles inside. If you are using candles, fix them securely in place with some hot wax.

IRIS LEAF TABLE MATS

Once the flowers have died down, iris leaves make an unusual material for weaving into eye-catching table mats. As the leaves are fairly broad, the mats do not take long to make. Imaginative yet simple, they provide a delightful decoration for outdoor entertaining, though they may not be able to survive very hot plates. Instead, use them for cold dishes, or make smaller mats and stand glasses on them.

MATERIALS

For each mat:

- strong carpet tape
- scissors
- 20 iris leaves, with their ends squared off neatly

1 Lay 10 of the trimmed iris leaves along a length of carpet tape to provide the warp.

2 Weave the remaining leaves in and out of these to form the weft. When you reach the bottom of the mat, tape that end of the warp to fix it firmly in place.

3 Fold the loose ends of the weft to the back of the mat, and then carefully weave them in to fix and neaten.

CHILDREN'S PARTY

Children love BRIGHT COLOURS, but that does not mean you have to be limited to primaries. You can take your cue from plastic straws and beakers, liquorice allsorts and SWEET WRAPPERS to create a clear pastel colour scheme. Spending a lot of money on a children's table setting is likely to go unnoticed: children will take far

greater delight in the SUGARED-ALMOND shades of the food itself, and you will be pleased to see it all eaten up or taken home as booty. Use sweets in a jar as a colourful table centrepiece, then invite the party guests to help themselves at the end of tea. Top ICED CUP CAKES with pastel-toned liquorice allsorts, then pile them decoratively high on a cake stand to make another eye-catching food idea. Add more colour with pretty GARLANDS OF SWEETS, and use bright cards for place names.

● Right: *A children's party is an ideal opportunity to create a table that is filled with colour.*

● Right: *These prettily wrapped sweets have been strung together with medium-gauge florist's wire, and then attached to the tablecloth. They make wonderful garlands for tables and side dressers alike. You could even add a small bow at each end of the sweets for a more lavish effect.*

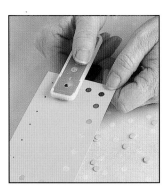

LACED NAME CARDS

Let the children help you make these decorative name cards – even a three-year-old will want to assist with this fun task.

MATERIALS

For each name card:
- coloured card, about 12 x 8cm/ 5 x 3in
- ruler
- pencil
- hole punch
- 1m/1yd cord
- coloured pen

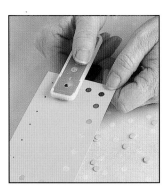

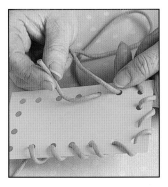

1 Mark out hole positions around the card, 2cm/¾in apart. Make the holes with the hole punch.

2 Lace the cord through the holes, finishing with a bow at one corner. Write the child's name in the centre.

HOME-MADE LETTER BISCUITS

Cut your favourite biscuit dough into the shape of each child's initial, and add decorative candy-striped bows once they are ready. They make exciting tasty treats for the children to take home.

MATERIALS

- paper
- pencil
- selection of newspapers or magazines (optional)
- scissors
- packet ready-mixed biscuit dough
- mixing bowl
- spoon
- rolling pin
- sharp kitchen knife
- baking tray
- spatula
- wire rack
- 15cm/6in ribbon for each biscuit

1 Draw large letters on a piece of paper and cut them out, or make the templates by enlarging letters from newspapers or magazines on a photocopier. Following the instructions on the packet, mix and roll out the biscuit dough. Place a letter on the dough and cut around it using a kitchen knife. Repeat for the other initials.

2 Cook on a greased baking tray according to packet instructions. Turn on to a wire rack to cool, then tie on ribbon bows.

EASTER FESTIVITY

Let Easter take on an East European flavour. In that part of the world, the feast was traditionally celebrated with nature-inspired decorations and specially prepared foods. Here, VIOLETS have set the colour scheme, combined

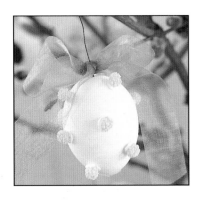

with AQUA, which happily mixes and matches in all its shades. Spring branches hung with decorated eggs are a Continental tradition, the BRANCHES bursting into leaf and BLOSSOM over the days of the celebration. Pussy-willow branches make a charming variation, creating a dramatic yet light and airy centrepiece. Violets are a delightful flower for SPRING decorations, and can be used for floral displays, for place decorations and to decorate the food. CRYSTALLIZED VIOLETS on the tall Russian bread and violet-patterned bone china complete the theme. Painted eggs have been used as decorations throughout.

● Right: *Violet blue and aqua make fresh alternatives to blues and yellows as a spring colour scheme.*

● Right: *Pashka is a favourite Russian Easter dish. To make it, mix equal parts of double cream and curd cheese, stir in dried, glacéed and crystallized fruit, and then turn into a cheesecloth-lined conical mould. Allow to drain thoroughly, then turn out and decorate with almonds and fresh violets.*

● Below: *Tiny mauve campanulas are wittily planted up in painted empty eggshells standing in simple white china egg cups to make a delicate display.*

● Above: *This tall Russian Easter bread (Italian pannetone may be substituted) has been drizzled with thick white royal icing, then scattered with crystallized violets, turquoise sugar roses and angelica.*

VIOLET POSIES

These delightful violet posies are easy to put together and make charming decorative party favours that guests will want to take home after the festivities. The delicate flowers quickly wilt once picked, so be sure to keep them in water (in tumblers, perhaps) until everyone is ready to go.

MATERIALS

For each posy:

- 3 long-stemmed leaves
- 15 violet blooms, tied with garden twine
- 23cm/9in turquoise ribbon
- approximately 15cm/6in gauzy purple ribbon for bows

1 Place long-stemmed leaves behind the violet flowers.

2 Spiral-bind the bunch with the turquoise ribbon and add a gauzy bow to the top, just under the violet blooms.

● Left: *Pale turquoise sugar-coated eggs are decoratively teamed with a turquoise-painted egg.*

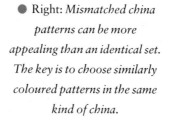

● Right: *Mismatched china patterns can be more appealing than an identical set. The key is to choose similarly coloured patterns in the same kind of china.*

EASTER EGG TREE

Any seasonal branches about to burst into bloom can be used for an Easter tree, which is hung with bought or home-decorated eggs.

MATERIALS

- secateurs
- 6 branches of pussy willow
- vase
- 7 blown eggs
- white matt emulsion and small artist's brush (optional)
- royal icing
- piping bag
- assorted small cake decorations, such as sugar flowers and mimosa balls
- florist's medium-gauge wire
- wire cutters
- assorted ribbon bows

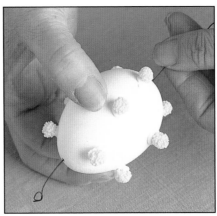

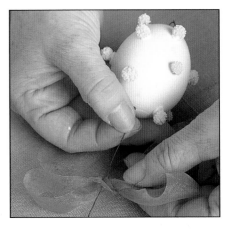

1 Cut the branches to length (even if no length needs taking off, trim the end of each branch). Place in a vase of water. If the eggs are brown, paint them with white matt emulsion and allow to dry. Use royal icing to fix the cake decorations to the eggs.

2 Cut a piece of wire about 15cm/6in long and make a loop at one end. Thread the wire through the egg and bend the loop flat against the bottom of the egg.

3 Thread the wire through a ribbon bow. Use the rest of the wire to make a hook for hanging the egg on the tree.

EASTER BASKET

A feather-lined basket of chocolate and decorated eggs makes a pretty table decoration, and the eggs can be handed out afterwards as Easter gifts.

MATERIALS

- 6 blown eggs
- white matt emulsion (optional)
- small artist's brush
- artist's pearl powder
- pale turquoise matt artist's paint
- basket
- white feathers
- pale blue feathers
- sugar eggs

1 If the eggs are brown, give them a coat of white matt emulsion and allow to dry.

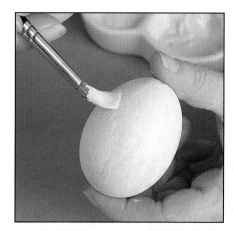

2 Mix a little pearl powder into the turquoise paint and paint on to cover the egg completely. Allow to dry.

3 Rub a little more dry pearl powder on to the egg. Fill the basket with feathers, then add the decorated and sugar eggs.

THANKSGIVING

The wonderfully soft GREY-GREENS and the MELLOW GOLDS of winter squashes provide a subtle colour scheme for a Thanksgiving celebration. A pile of PUMPKINS forms a striking centrepiece, while small hollowed-out squashes become soup bowls. Dried-oregano topiary trees offer fragrant focal points at either end of the table, and imitate the gently drying and falling

leaves outside. Real AUTUMN leaves are cut to smaller leaf shapes and used as printing blocks to add decoration to a plain tablecloth. Runner beans, symbolic of a FRUITFUL HARVEST, are used as place decorations for the soup course, their SOFT GREEN skins complementing the colours of the pumpkins and squashes. Where the guests outnumber available dining chairs, garden chairs can be "softened" or a disparate set of chairs co-ordinated by making button-on slips to fit over the backs.

● Right: *Turn squashes into soup bowls and pumpkins into decorations to create an evocative autumn table.*

SQUASH SOUP BOWLS

Hollowed-out squashes make unusual seasonal soup bowls, and are especially appropriate for serving delicious steaming pumpkin soup.

MATERIALS

- squashes
- sharp kitchen knife
- metal spoon

1 Cut the top third from each squash and a sliver from the bottom so that the bowl stands flat. Using a metal spoon, carefully hollow out the seeds and enough of the flesh to create an attractive bowl for the soup.

BUTTON-DOWN CHAIR BACKS

A smart way to co-ordinate unmatched seating, fabric chair backs could not be easier to make. You could even make several sets in different colours to accompany different schemes, or mix and match fabrics within the same set.

MATERIALS

For each chair:

- fabric the width of the widest part of the chair back plus 8cm/3in, and twice the desired depth
- scissors
- sewing machine (optional)
- needle
- thread
- 2 buttons

1 Hem the bottom edges of each cover by hand or machine. Make buttonholes near the bottom of one side and 15cm/6in in from the side edges. Fold in half, wrong sides together, and stitch the side seams. Turn right side out and stitch the buttons in position.

LEAF-STENCILLED CLOTH

Here is a witty way to hand-print a cloth with a seasonal motif. Use an autumn leaf mounted on to a wood block or thick card as the printing block, in order to produce a veined effect.

MATERIALS

- wooden leaf shape or thick card
- scalpel
- cutting mat
- clearly veined autumn leaf
- all-purpose glue
- cork
- fabric paint
- saucer
- newspaper
- tablecloth

1 Place the wooden leaf shape or card template on to a large leaf (for the template, draw a leaf on to the card and cut it out using a sharp scalpel).

2 Carefully cut out the leaf shape using a scalpel. Glue this leaf to the wood block or the card template to use as a stamp.

3 Glue the cork to the other side of the wood to make a handle. Dip into a saucer of fabric paint and work off excess colour by stamping it on to a piece of newspaper. Stamp on to the cloth at regular intervals.

● Left: *Pumpkins at varying stages of ripeness can be piled one on top of the other and sat on silver-grey reindeer moss for a pleasingly toned arrangement. For an evening party – especially at Hallowe'en – you could even cut a "lid" from the top pumpkin, scoop out the seeds and flesh, and then cut shapes in the skin, before placing one or more candles inside.*

VALENTINE DINNER

When romance is in the air, ambience is paramount. Set the scene for a romantic dinner for two with PURE WHITE AND PASTEL PINK, open the champagne (pink, of course) and switch on the music. Scent the air with RICHLY PERFUMED

FLOWERS such as lilac and tuber roses, and burn white beeswax candles. Make some heart-shaped chocolates, and then gift-wrap them as part of the table decoration, placing them in a BLUSH-PINK FROSTED bowl. The palest pink with white makes for the most elegant of schemes, especially when given the extra "bite" of another pastel to lend definition. For this table, a TOUCH OF SAPPHIRE and punctuations of aqua add just the amount of coolness needed. As the sun goes down, the pinks will deepen, and the whites will become more moody.

● Right: *Hearts and flowers, candles and home-made confections in pastels and white add up to a romantic dinner for two.*

● Right: *Heart-shaped cheeses set upon a glass cake stand and decorated with berries provide a decorative finale to a romantic meal. The arrangement of the cheeses to make a four-leaved clover is also a lucky charm, while the pink stem of the cake stand blends beautifully with the rest of the table setting.*

ROMANTIC POSIES

Scented flowers are a must for romantic arrangements. Some garden roses have the inimitable scent of summer, but most florist's roses have little or no perfume. Compensate by adding fragrant tuber roses and lilac, if it is in season.

MATERIALS

- scissors
- 2 heads of white roses
- 2 heads of tuber roses
- 1 head of white lavender
- 3 heads of white ranunculus
- lustre-glass vase
- 3 sprays of pink peppercorns

1 Cut the stems so that the blooms will rest on the rim of the vase. Place in the vase, then add pink peppercorns to emphasize the blush-pink colour scheme.

APPLIQUÉ CUPID CLOTH

For a delightfully romantic table dressing, sew engaging cupids to each corner of a silk organza cloth, then decorate with tiny pearls. Calculate the size of cloth needed, then turn in a small hem all round, press and slip-stitch. Do this as neatly as you can, or the stitches will be visible on the surface of the fine cloth.

MATERIALS

- tracing paper
- pencil
- paper
- scissors
- pins
- lace or spotted muslin, about 60 x 15cm/24 x 6in
- needle
- white thread
- silk organza or similar fabric
- 28 seed-pearl beads

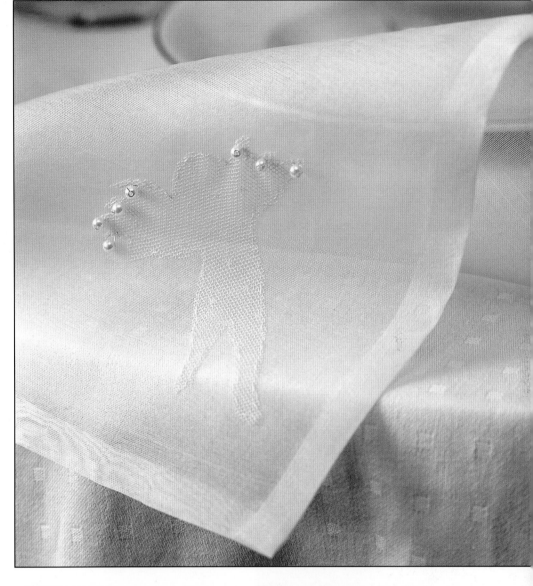

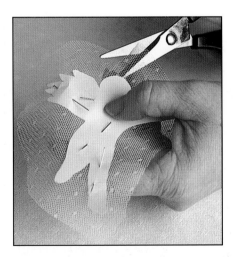

1 Trace the template from the back of the book. Pin to the lace or muslin and cut out.

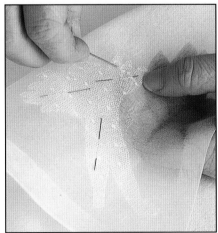

2 Hand-sew one cupid to each corner of the cloth using tiny running stitches.

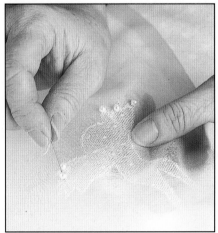

3 Sew three seed-pearl beads to the wing tips of each cupid.

PASTEL MERINGUES

A cut-glass cake stand piled high with meringues in pretty pastel shades – some heart-shaped, others decorated with silver balls – makes a decorative centrepiece before the components are sampled at the end of the meal.

MATERIALS

- 3 egg whites
- whisk
- 2 bowls
- 175g/6oz icing sugar
- mauve and pink food colouring
- piping bag
- baking tray with baking parchment to fit
- silver or sugar balls to decorate
- spatula
- cut-glass cake stand

1 Preheat the oven to 120°C/250°F/gas mark ½. Whisk the egg whites until they are really stiff, then fold in the icing sugar a little at a time. Whisk the mixture over a very low heat for a few seconds to give a firm mixture for piping. Divide into two batches and tint separately with mauve and pink food colouring.

2 Pipe small heart shapes and meringue shapes on to the baking parchment.

3 Decorate the shapes with silver or sugar balls. Bake for one hour until the meringues lift off the parchment easily. Allow to cool, then pile on to a cake stand.

WHITE-CHOCOLATE HEARTS

Gift-wrap a pair of mouthwatering chocolate hearts for each place setting as romantic party favours. The glassine paper used to wrap the hearts creates a pretty, "misty" effect; it should be available from department stores or good suppliers of kitchenware.

MATERIALS

- good-quality white chocolate, 100g/3½oz for each heart
- bowl
- saucepan
- wooden spoon
- baking tin
- aluminium foil
- 10cm/4in heart-shaped metal cutters
- metal spoon
- gold or silver balls to decorate
- glassine paper to wrap
- fine linen string
- scissors

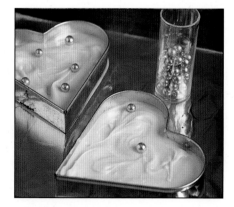

1 Break up the chocolate and melt it slowly in a bowl set over a pan of boiling water, stirring all the time with a wooden spoon. Remove the bowl from the heat.

2 Line the baking tin with aluminium foil, and place the metal cutters on the foil. Using the metal spoon, drop the melted chocolate into the cutters.

3 Decorate with gold or silver balls and leave to set. Wrap the whole heart, with the cutter, in glassine paper and tie with fine linen string.

WHITE WEDDING

Dress a wedding table all in white, just like the bride. This one is clothed in several layers of muslin topped by a FROTH OF TULLE. Quite apart from its relevance to the occasion, white is always a good colour to choose for any entertaining where the guests outnumber the

normal dinner service, because it can so easily be MIXED AND MATCHED with extras borrowed from friends and family.

WHITE ON WHITE, cream on cream, or even a combination of both works well, lending a unity to shapes that do not match: the colour variations add depth to the finished scheme. Here, the decorations have been kept organic – fruit and flowers in GREEN AND WHITE for a look that retains a natural sense of peace. It is also fun to enhance the romantic theme with heart-frosted glasses and a pair of cherubs.

● Right: *Add romantic touches to a table dressed in white for a delightful wedding theme.*

ORCHID NAPKIN TIES

The elegant lines of clean white orchid heads make for pretty yet smart napkin ties – the perfect complement to pure white linen.

MATERIALS

For each napkin:

- 25cm (10in) narrow off-white ribbon
- 2 leaves
- 1 orchid head or other similar-sized white flower

1 Loosely pleat the napkin to fit on the plate. If the napkin is far too long for the plate, start by making a large tuck in the centre so it is about the same length as the plate, then loosely pleat it to make a fan.

2 Loosely tie the narrow ribbon around the middle of the napkin.

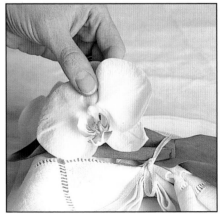

3 Carefully tuck the leaves into the ribbon, then add the flower.

TULIP BOUQUET ARRANGEMENT

Where a wide-necked container such as this soup tureen offers little support, one of the simplest solutions is to tie the flowers into a generous posy and stand them in the bowl. This elegant bouquet of two types of white tulip was made especially for the table setting, but the bride's own bouquet could just as easily be put into a beautiful container after the ceremony, transforming it into an exquisite centrepiece.

MATERIALS

- generous bunches of white tulips and white parrot tulips
- bunch of bear's grass
- garden raffia
- scissors
- white soup tureen

1 Make a bunch of tulips, mixing the varieties and interspersing them with bear's grass. Cross the tulip stems over each other diagonally to make a spiral, to make a fuller-looking bunch.

2 Using garden raffia, tie the bunch firmly. Trim the ends of the raffia.

3 Place the tied bunch in a soup tureen filled with fresh water.

HEART-FROSTED GLASSES

Frosting glasses is quick and easy, but the technique is all too often restricted to the rims. On romantic occasions, take the idea a step further by frosting a heart on the side of each glass. The frosting is remarkably resilient and will last well throughout the party. Afterwards, you will need plenty of hot, soapy water to remove it. Here, a delicate bow tied around the stem of the glass adds a pretty finishing touch.

MATERIALS

- 2 saucers
- 1 egg white, beaten
- small artist's brush
- glasses
- caster sugar
- short lengths of off-white ribbon for bows

1 Dip the brush into the beaten egg white and paint a heart shape on to the glass. You will not see much at this stage, so fill in the shape with plenty of egg white.

2 Sprinkle caster sugar on to the painted heart; it will stick to the egg white. Shake off the excess sugar.

3 Dip the glass rim into the egg white, and then into the sugar for a frosted rim. Shake off the excess sugar. Tie a bow to the stem of the glass.

CARVED PEAR CENTREPIECE

The natural beauty of fruit makes it perfect for table decoration. Conference pears become elegant sculptures when selectively peeled to reveal stripes of creamy flesh.

MATERIALS
- 3 pears
- sharp paring knife
- fresh lemon juice
- tazza or food stand

1 Firm, slightly underripe pears carve best. Holding the large end of the pear, carefully remove strips of skin.

2 Coat the peeled areas with lemon juice to prevent the flesh from discolouring. Arrange the pears on the tazza.

TULLE PARTY FAVOURS

Team the party favours with the tablecloth by making them in matching tulle, but line them with white tissue paper instead of muslin to give support.

MATERIALS

For each favour:
- white tissue paper, 15cm/6in square
- tulle, 15cm/6in square
- silver dragées or similar sweets
- 15cm/6in narrow off-white ribbon

1 Lay the square of tissue paper on top of the square of tulle. Place the silver sweets in the centre, then gather up and tie with the ribbon.

TRADITIONAL CHRISTMAS

For a truly traditional Christmas, hark back to an era before the invention of tinsel and baubles when NATURAL, ORGANIC materials provided the decoration, the textures and the evocative SCENTS. Draw inspiration from the Elizabethans, who created a festive ambience rich with the AROMAS of oranges and bay, and of

heady spices such as CINNAMON AND CLOVES. These ingredients can be the starting point of an elegant colour scheme, substituting RUSSETS AND ORANGES for the more usual reds. Supplement the rich mood by looking for exotic fruits and vegetables like pomegranates, Chinese lanterns and artichokes, and highlight them with voluptuous bunches of black grapes. Use rusty metal vases, RICH BRASS or AMBER GLASS plates, then add a hint of gold for the Midas touch.

● Right: *At Christmas, let nature do the decorating, adding colour with fruit and flowers, and scent with spices and beeswax.*

● Right: *Dress elegantly etched glasses with golden tassels tied to the stems with lengths of golden twine to give them a sense of celebration. If the stems of the glasses are not "ribbed", as here, and the tassels tend to slip down, secure the twine with tiny pieces of invisible tape.*

BROCADE PARTY FAVOURS

A charming brocade bag tied up with silken cord is gift enough indeed; it can also contain a small present for each guest and be decoratively placed next to each setting.

MATERIALS

For each bag:

● brocade, 15 x 60cm/ 6 x 24in
● scissors
● needle
● thread
● small gift
● 20cm/8in silk cord
● rosebud (optional)

1 Cut two pieces of brocade, each measuring 15 x 30cm/ 6 x 12in. Fold down a 5cm/ 2in hem at the top edge of each piece and stitch the hem.

2 With right sides facing, stitch a seam around three sides, leaving the hemmed edges at the top open. Turn to the right side, fill with a small gift and tie the cord around the bag. Decorate with a rosebud if desired.

ADVENT CANDLE CENTREPIECE

Traditionally, the four Advent candles are burned for an hour on each Sunday leading up to Christmas. On the first Sunday, one candle is burned for an hour. On the second Sunday it is burned alongside the second candle, and so on. This lovely idea inspired this centre-piece, which could just as well have all its candles burning on one occasion.

MATERIALS

- florist's foam brick
- plate
- 4 church or beeswax candles
- bunch of tree ivy
- secateurs or scissors
- picture framer's gilt wax
- fine wire
- wire cutters
- 10 Chinese lanterns

1 Soak the florist's foam brick in water and set it on a plate. Carefully push the candles into the foam.

2 Cut the tree ivy stems to size and push them into the florist's foam. Gild the berries with picture framer's gilt wax.

3 Pass a wire through the base of each Chinese lantern and then twist the ends together. Push the twisted wire ends into the florist's foam base to fix the Chinese lanterns in position.

149

SEASONAL GARLAND

Natural decorations are by far the most beautiful and this easily made garland can be placed on a mantelpiece or adapted for use as a door wreath.

MATERIALS

- plastic garland cradle or chicken wire, the length of desired finished piece and three times the width
- wire cutters (optional)
- 3 florist's foam bricks
- large bunch of tree ivy
- florist's medium-gauge stub wires
- picture framer's gilt wax

For every 15cm/6in of garland:

- artichoke
- 2 dried oranges
- cinnamon sticks
- gold cord
- scissors

1 First make the base. If using a garland cradle, fill each section with florist's foam, then soak in water. Join the cradle sections together. If using chicken wire, roll it into a long sausage filled with florist's foam and cut to size. Soak in water, then form into a circle. Push tree ivy sprigs into the foam to make a full base.

2 Pass a florist's wire through the base of each artichoke and dried orange, then fix these in position around the garland. Gild the ivy berries, the dried oranges and the tips of the artichoke leaves using picture framer's gilt wax.

3 Tie the cinnamon sticks into bunches of two or three using gold cord. Fix a wire through the cord and then fix this into the garland.

FORMAL URN ARRANGEMENT

Urns always give flower arrangements a dignified look and encourage professional results. Aim to have some material that drapes gracefully and some that gives structure to the arrangement. Here, russet roses and calla lilies are set against tree ivy with gilded berries.

MATERIALS

- florist's foam brick
- scissors
- metal urn
- large bunch of tree ivy
- secateurs
- picture framer's gilt wax
- 5 calla lilies
- 5 russet roses

1 Soak the florist's foam in water. Cut it to fit the urn and place inside. Trim the tree ivy to length and gild the berries using the picture framer's gilt wax. Use the ivy to make a full base arrangement.

2 Trim the calla lilies to length and place them in the arrangement. Repeat with the roses to complete, making sure they are all at slightly different angles.

MODERN CHRISTMAS

A sharp, modern Christmas table teams spicy orange with BURNISHED GOLD. Set against a strong structure of large but elegant shapes, there is scope for adding some tasteful embellishments with plenty of SEASONAL SPARKLE. A generously

sized glass vase that is piled high with KUMQUATS makes an innovative centrepiece, offset by a stemmed dish of SHIMMERING ORANGE and golden baubles. But the real ingenuity comes into play with the detail: glasses laced with fine gold wire, then given a golden rim stripe punctuated by MINIATURE JEWELS, and plates decorated with more stick-on jewels, gold-painted leaves and bead-trimmed napkins. Brass underplates topped by glass dinner plates, along with brass cutlery and GOLD LUSTRE coffee cups, continue the gold theme.

● Right: *Express the Christmas spirit by adding decorative treats, such as gift-wrapped party favours and foil-wrapped sweets.*

● Right: *Floating gerbera petals add co-ordinated decoration to a pretty glass finger bowl. You could use any type of petals for this idea, either keeping to one colour or using a range of shades for a really vibrant effect.*

STARRY TABLECLOTH

A white voile overcloth can be given the Midas touch with the addition of simple six-pointed golden stars.

MATERIALS

- circular object, about 7.5cm/3in in diameter
- card
- pencil
- ruler
- white voile to fit the table and hang down the sides
- gold paint
- small artist's brush

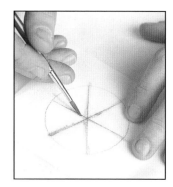

1 Place the circular object on the card and draw around it. Draw three lines for the star to make six equal sections.

2 Place the card under the voile and carefully paint the star shape on the cloth, using gold paint. Repeat randomly over the whole surface of the tablecloth. Allow to dry.

DECORATED GLASSES

At Christmas, dress your wine glasses for dinner. Lace fine gold wire around them, and add jewel-punctuated golden stripes and strings of gold beads to create simple yet striking decorations for glassware. A stick-on jewel added to the golden rim completes this lavish yet elegantly understated look.

MATERIALS

- fine beading wire
- stemmed glasses
- all-purpose glue
- masking tape
- card
- gold spray paint
- scalpel and cutting mat
- steel ruler
- stick-on jewels

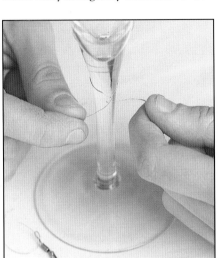

1 "Lace" fine beading wire around the stem and bowl of a glass. Tie the wire to fix in place, and add a spot of glue.

2 Stick a length of masking tape (long enough to go around the glass) on to a piece of card and spray it gold. Use a scalpel and steel ruler to cut it into thin strips. Fix a strip to each glass near the rim, and trim with a stick-on jewel.

GIFT-WRAPPED PARTY FAVOURS

Wrapping offers great scope for adding impact to co-ordinated table settings. These gold-painted white tissue parcels are a simple solution, and look highly effective in orange glass bowls.

MATERIALS

- gifts
- white tissue paper
- gold paint
- small artist's brush
- gold organza ribbon
- gold-painted leaves (as for place cards opposite)
- fine gold ribbon

1 Wrap up the gift, then paint gold dots and strokes on the tissue paper parcel. Tie it up with organza ribbon, and decorate it with gold leaves and fine gold ribbon.

BEADED NAPKINS

Trim orange linen napkins with a row of tiny running stitches in co-ordinating tapestry wool, and finish off with fine orange beads at each corner if you wish.

MATERIALS

- napkins
- orange tapestry wool
- tapestry needle
- scissors
- 24 small orange beads (optional)

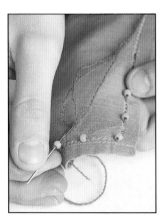

1 Make small running stitches in wool around the napkin border, threading on beads where desired. Here, five evenly spaced beads finish off each corner.

156

GOLDEN PLACE CARDS

Touches of gold will turn ordinary small, round-cornered cards available from stationers into seasonal place cards.

MATERIALS

- small, round-cornered cards
- ruler
- scalpel
- cutting mat
- gold pen
- stick-on jewels (optional)
- stems of foliage
- gold paint
- small artist's brush
- all-purpose glue

1 Score across the mid-way point of the card using the ruler and scalpel. Fold the card at this point. Write the guest's name on the front in gold, and add a stick-on jewel if you like.

2 Paint the leaves on the stems of foliage with gold paint, and use to decorate the card. Fix in place and glue.

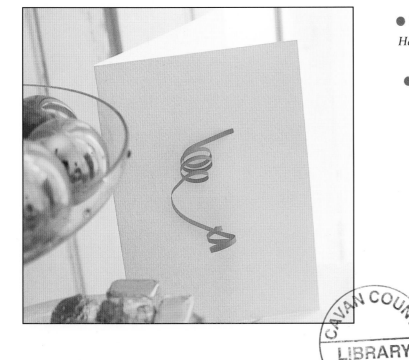

● Left: *Even the simplest cards can enhance the table setting. Here, a white card is decorated with a twirl of paper ribbon.*

● Below: *Red and gold baubles in a tall glass dish create a festive feel.*

INDEX

Page numbers in *italic* refer to the illustrations

AUTHOR'S ACKNOWLEDGEMENTS

My very special thanks go to:
JANE NEWDICK (*Easter Festivity, Valentine Dinner, Thanksgiving, Outdoor Party, Out of Africa, Children's Party*) and ANDREA SPENCER (*White Magic, Simply Natural, Modern Minimalism, Fun with Colour, Sun-filled Style, Modern Christmas, Shaker Styling*) – their many and varied talents bring a wonderful range of beautiful and innovative ideas to *Table Settings*. To JENNY NORTON, who so effectively pulled the directory sections together. To POLLY WREFORD whose breathtaking photographs so exquisitely capture the mood of each table setting, and whose immense good humour and unstinting hard work kept us all going. To CLARE NICHOLSON for her supporting calm , and for so skilfully smoothing the book through the production process. To LISA TAI for her most elegant and sensitive design that so beautifully complements all the ideas in the book. The pictures on page 12 were taken by Peter Williams (right), Debbie Patterson (left), and the picture on page 13 by Spike Powell.

Our thanks also go to the following people who kindly lent products for the pictures:

Maryse Boxer and Carolyn Quartermaine, Chez Joseph, 26 Sloane Street, London SW1X 7LQ; tel: 0171 245 9493 (*Cutlery and napkins*)

Genevieve Lethu, 132 Brompton Road, London SW3 1HJ; tel: 0171 581 9939 (*Glasses*)

McCloud & Co., 269 Wandsworth Bridge Road, London SW6 2TX; tel: 0171 371 7151 (*Chairs*)

Rita Martinez, 775 Fulham Road, London SW6 5HA; tel: 0171 731 8617 (*Upholstered chair*)

The Linen Shop, Harvey Nichols, Knightsbridge, London SW1; tel: 0171 236 5000 (*Linens*)

Cameron Shaw, 279 New King's Road, London SW6; tel: 0171 371 8175 (*Topiary*)